MANSFIELD-RICHLAND COUNTY PUB
DISCARD

MAY - - 1997

was also the first time the family had a living room, and Father Scott bought a new set of furniture for it.

As they grew up, the Scott children became more aware that there were places that black children couldn't go, and that white children and white people were treated better than black people. Coretta noticed this when the black children would go to the drugstore, which was owned by a white man, to buy an ice-cream cone. The black children had to go to a side door, not the front door, and had to wait until all the white children were served. Then, whatever flavor the black children asked for, the man would give them the flavor *he* wanted—usually what he had an excess of—and charged them the same amount that he charged the white children.

When things like this happened, naturally black children would run to their parents and ask why this was so. And the parents, knowing that this time would come, would always patiently explain, "Honey, it's just the way things are. But remember, you are just as good as anyone else." Coretta's mother said the same thing, but added very firmly, "You get an education and try to be somebody. Then you won't have to be kicked around by anybody, and you won't have to depend on anyone for your livelihood."[2]

SECONDARY SCHOOL

After they finished the sixth grade, it was time for the children to go to secondary school. There was a black high school in the community, but Coretta's mother wanted her children to go to the best school there was.

She arranged for the children to go to Lincoln High School, located ten miles away in Marion, because it was an unusual school. It had been started

The school that the Scott children attended was in an unpainted wooden building with one big room. In this room, classes were held with more than one hundred children in the first through sixth grades. They had no real blackboards; parts of the walls were painted black and used as blackboards. And the bathrooms were outside.

Despite the grim facilities, the teachers were very dedicated. In those days it wasn't necessary to have a college education to teach in black schools, but the two black women who were the teachers in Coretta's school were highly educated. One of Coretta's teachers, Mrs. Mattie Bennett, encouraged both Coretta and Edythe because she recognized their eagerness to learn.

One of the activities that young Coretta was involved in was singing. Whenever the county supervisor would come to inspect their school, the students would give a presentation. Coretta was always asked to lead songs, sing solos, or recite poetry.

Coretta and her sister and brother enjoyed going to school. Their parents had not been able to finish school and realized how much they had missed. Therefore, the Scotts were determined that their children would get an education. Coretta's mother advised, "You want clothes and other things now, but once you have an education, if you still want these things, you can get them. The most important thing now is to get an education."[1] Coretta's mother had only been able to go to school until the fourth grade, attending only three months a year because she had to work on her family's farm.

When Coretta was ten years old, her father rented another house, and the family moved in. This house was bigger, with six rooms, and it was the first time Coretta and Edythe had a room of their own! It

Two

Education

Young Coretta, Edythe, and Obie attended a one-room schoolhouse in Heiberger, three miles from home. Rain or shine, they walked to and from school every day.

Coretta realized quite early that there was a difference between the school they went to and that of the white children. First of all, the white children had a bus that took them to school. That bus would pass the Scott children, splattering dust or mud on them as they were walking to school. Coretta resented that. The white children's school was in a brick building, and probably had different classrooms for each grade, a library, free textbooks for the children, and other kinds of supplies that were needed for teaching and learning. The black children's school, on the other hand, had no library and very few books. In fact, the children had to pay for their regular textbooks. The white children attended school for nine months a year; the black children went for seven months a year.

Although Coretta grew up during the Great Depression, her family's hard work meant that they had a place to live, food to eat, and clothing to wear. While they were still young, the Scott children learned the value and rewards of working hard. Their father made them get up early, even if they had nothing to do. Usually, they had plenty to do, though, because he taught them when they were quite young to keep busy.

As young children, Coretta, Edythe, and Obie labored in the cotton fields with the hired men, hoeing and chopping the cotton. By working this way, they made their own money to help with their school needs.

Church activities were a big part of the community's life. Because most of the people in the town were related in some way, going to church on Sunday was like a big family gathering. Everybody wore their best clothes, and some people came long distances—riding in wagons, or walking, the way the Scott family did when Obadiah was not in town. The church was about four miles from their home. Coretta enjoyed the atmosphere at church, with her two grandfathers presiding over the activities.

The town they lived in was, of course, all black. From a young age, everyone was aware of segregation, and knew that there were certain things they would not be permitted to do because of the color of their skin. But because many families had owned their land for three generations, there was a lot of pride, dignity, and self-esteem among the people. For young Coretta, having such a big family meant that there were always other children to play with: cousins, and half uncles and half aunts from Grandfather Scott's second marriage.

Jeff and Cora Scott were hardworking people, who had both been born just after the slaves were freed. They also worked with logs and timber, and they sold enough to buy a farm. Jeff and Cora had thirteen children together, and after Cora's death, Jeff remarried, to a woman named Fannie Burroughs, and had twelve more children.

Jeff Scott owned three hundred acres of land, which made him an important man in his community. All the black people in Marion called him "Mr. Scott." He held many positions of responsibility, including Sunday school superintendent, in their church, Mount Taber A.M.E. (African Methodist Episcopal) Zion Church. His positions required him to travel to church conferences and meetings, and he was able to see what life was like in other places. When he was sixty-eight years old, he was killed in an automobile accident.

Coretta's Grandfather McMurry, her mother's father, was born just before the slaves were freed. He was part American Indian, and had fair skin and straight black hair. He had never gone to school, but had a rich vocabulary and had taught himself to read the Bible, which was all he read. He became quite an expert at interpreting the Bible, and people considered him an authority. He was highly respected in the community by both blacks and whites. Grandfather McMurry was also a strict man who believed that children should be seen and not heard. When Coretta, Edythe, and Obie went to visit they would play very, very quietly outside. If they made a noise, he would come out and threaten to whip them! The children were afraid of him, so they didn't talk to him too much. Grandmother McMurry was a loving woman who enjoyed flowers and working in her garden. She also made most of the Scott children's clothes.

used it to carry logs and timber for his boss. Because he was the only black man who owned a truck, the poorer white men resented him because they saw him as competition. He never ran away, even when they threatened to kill him. He believed that if you look a man in the eye, he won't hurt you. Scott chose to think the best about people. If people were bad, it was because conditions made them that way. But he knew he could be in danger. Many times when he left home to go into the dark woods to haul lumber, he'd say to Coretta's mother, "I may not get back."[1]

Coretta's father also learned how to cut hair, so in the evenings and on weekends, he would make money from the men who would come for haircuts. Coretta's mother also helped him when there were a lot of customers. Since they had some land, they grew potatoes, corn, peas, and other vegetables, and had cows, chickens, and pigs. This was the source of the family's food. Coretta, her mother, Edythe, and Obie were all responsible for taking care of the garden and the animals.

Coretta's mother was part American Indian. She was a woman who placed a great value on education, because she had only been able to go to school until the fourth grade. She was very resentful of the way black people were treated, much more so than Coretta's father.

Coretta's grandfather and grandmother on her father's side were Jeff and Cora Scott. Coretta was named after her father's mother, and when Coretta was growing up, her mother often told her that she was very much like her grandmother Cora, who had been a very strong and determined woman. Coretta never knew her grandmother Cora, though, because she had died at the age of forty, before Coretta was born.

("Colored" and "Negro" were the terms used then to describe black people. Today, non-white Americans of African descent are referred to as "African-American" or "black.")

But Coretta Scott's family was proud, strong, and hardworking. So for generations, despite the obstacles that were placed in their way, they worked hard so that they could live comfortably.

Coretta's father, Obadiah Scott, and her mother, Bernice McMurry Scott, were married in 1920. After they were married, Obadiah built a house for them on his father's farm, and it was in this house that Coretta was born. This unpainted wooden house had a front porch and two big rooms, a kitchen and a bedroom, inside. The kitchen had plain wooden floors, a big table, some chairs with cane seats, and a big iron woodburning stove for cooking. The bedroom had two double beds, a dresser, a wardrobe, and an open fireplace for heat. Outside, behind the house, there was a well which provided water.

The Scott house also had a very important piece of furniture: a Victrola (the original record player). To go with it, the family also had a collection of records which included hymns, sermons, popular songs, and jazz music. Coretta, her older sister Edythe, and younger brother Obie all enjoyed listening to these records with their parents. There were also a few books in the house, and their mother would read stories and recite nursery rhymes to them such as "Mary Had a Little Lamb" and "Humpty Dumpty." When they were older, the children would read the books over and over.

Coretta's father used all his skills to get ahead. When he and Bernice got married, he had a job at one of the local sawmills, and earned three dollars a day. Slowly, he saved enough money to buy a truck and

One

Growing Up

On the map of the United States, the state of Alabama is located just above Florida and one state to the west of Georgia. There is a little farm town, located between Montgomery and Birmingham, called Marion. A few miles outside of Marion is where Coretta Scott was born on April 27, 1927.

In those days, black people in the South were treated very unfairly by whites. After slavery was abolished in America in 1865, the treatment of blacks was better for a while. But in 1881, southern states began making laws and rulings designed to keep blacks from voting, from getting a basic education, owning land, or having a business. They also made laws requiring that black people be segregated from white people as much as possible. Black people and white people were not allowed to sit together in buses, trains, or theaters; to use the same water fountains or public rest rooms; or to even enter public buildings by the same door. In all public places, there were signs reading WHITES ONLY and COLORED ONLY.

cause. This is where their strength came from: they believed in their struggle.

Following her husband's death, Coretta Scott King—often under criticism of people who thought she should be pursuing other social interests—dedicated herself to building the Martin Luther King, Jr., Center for Nonviolent Social Change, and to having January 15, King's birthday, declared a national holiday. She succeeded in both efforts. Our calendars note that January 15 is the national holiday commemorating Martin Luther King, Jr.'s, birthday. The King Center, completed in 1981, is located in Atlanta, Georgia, and includes Ebenezer Baptist Church, Dr. King's birth home, his crypt, and the Freedom Hall Complex. Thousands of people visit the center each year to learn about Martin Luther King, Jr., and the Civil Rights Movement, and to study the philosophy of nonviolence.

Coretta Scott King has always been a sensitive, strong, intelligent woman. She never planned to marry a minister; she had intended to be a concert singer, and was pursuing a degree in music at the New England Conservatory of Music when she met Martin Luther King, Jr. Deciding to marry him changed her plans. . . .

First, she had to adjust to the role of being a minister's wife. Before she could get used to *that* role, she became a mother. Then before she could get used to *that* role, the civil rights protests began, and her husband became one of its strongest leaders. His work led him to become famous all over the world. During those years, she had to raise her four children, run a house which was visited at all hours by people from all over the world, and help with her husband's work—which sometimes involved her making concert appearances all over the country.

As the wife of a famous man who fought against injustice, Coretta King had to be very understanding and often very brave. Many times she did prove that she was just as brave as her husband. When her home was bombed while she and her infant daughter were in it, Coretta King refused to run. Her husband was repeatedly arrested, jailed, and attacked, and Coretta King provided him with the unlimited moral support he needed to continue his work. After Dr. King was brutally assassinated, she picked up where he left off, and continued to travel around the world teaching people about peace and brotherhood.

Coretta King's strength and control impressed visitors and friends. Often, reporters who came to speak to her husband stayed to interview her. In many of these interviews, she would speak of how vulnerable her whole family was to danger. But they were committed to the cause of civil rights, and were willing to make great personal sacrifices for this

Introduction
A Lady with a Commitment

When you hear the name Coretta Scott King, you think of the woman who was the wife of civil rights leader Dr. Martin Luther King, Jr. You remember her from the photographs you have seen: the woman holding his hand as he leads one of his many marches, the woman surrounded by four small, well-behaved children, or the strong, silent woman wearing the black veil at his funeral.

Perhaps you may not think of Coretta Scott King so readily as a civil rights activist (an activist is a person who believes in the use of action, instead of silence, as a way to achieve results). Or as a singer, with a talented soprano voice. Or as the person who was responsible for establishing the Martin Luther King, Jr., Center for Nonviolent Social Change, Inc. in Atlanta. Or as the person who was responsible for getting Martin Luther King's birthday declared a national holiday.

This book will introduce you to *that* Coretta Scott King.

This book is dedicated
—with humble thanks—
to
R. LESLIE GOURSE
and
DAVID J. GARROW
who each graciously accepted the sudden
selection as Handpicked Role Model
and provided unfailing, unselfish, and
good-natured support;
AND
—with love—
to
all young people
who know that reading is their own
private magic by which they can
travel to unlimited heights

Contents

Introduction
A Lady with
a Commitment 9

One
Growing Up 13

Two
Education 18

Three
Courtship and Marriage 35

Four
Early Years with Martin Luther King, Jr. 49

Five
Working for Civil Rights 75

Six
Continuing the Work 102

Source Notes 122

Bibliography 124

Index 126

Photographs copyright ©: Antiochiana, Antioch College: p. 1; UPI/Bettmann Newsphotos: pp. 2, 3, 4, 5, 11, 13, 14, 15; Pictorial Parade: pp. 6, 10, 12 (Tim Boxer); Flip Schulke: pp. 7, 8, 9; Gamma-Liaison: p. 16 (Alan Weiner).

Library of Congress Cataloging-in-Publication Data
Patrick, Diane.
Coretta Scott King / by Diane Patrick.
p. cm.—(An Impact biography)
Includes bibliographical references and index.
Summary: Examines the life and work of Coretta Scott King.
ISBN 0-531-13005-3
1. King, Coretta Scott, 1927– —Juvenile literature. 2. King, Martin Luther, Jr., 1929–1968—Juvenile literature. 3. Afro-Americans—Biography—Juvenile literature. 4. Civil rights workers—United States—Biography—Juvenile literature. [1. King, Coretta Scott, 1927– . 2. King, Martin Luther, Jr., 1929–1968. 3. Afro-Americans—Biography.] I. Title.
E185.97.K47P36 1991
323'.092—dc20
[B]   91-17032 CIP AC

Copyright © 1991 by Diane Patrick
All rights reserved
Printed in the United States of America
5 4 3 2

CORETTA SCOTT KING

DIANE PATRICK

An Impact Biography
Franklin Watts
New York   London   Toronto   Sydney

Coretta Scott King

after the Civil War by the American Missionary Association. At that time, there were no schools at all in the South for black children, all of whom were former slaves. Originally, the teachers at Lincoln were white missionaries who were sent there from northern states. These teachers were very brave people who truly wanted to help the children. When Coretta went there, half of the faculty was black and half was white, and the teachers lived together in dormitories provided by the school. Only a few of the white people of Marion made friends with the teachers. The rest of the white residents refused to have anything to do with them and called them terrible names because they mixed with black people and taught black children. But Lincoln High had a strong tradition of service to others, and this tradition was passed on to its students.

Not too many parents were able to send their children to high school, because in a farming community like theirs, a family lost a helper when the children were at school. In the Scott children's case, Mother and Father Scott had to pay tuition of $4.50 per year for each child, which was a lot of money for them. And because Lincoln was too far from home for the Scott children to be able to walk every day, they had to stay with a black family in Marion. This too cost money. The white children in the area had the convenience of being taken by bus to their high school in Marion.

In Marion, Coretta had more encounters with prejudice than she had ever experienced before. Sometimes, when the black children walked to school, white teenagers would come down the street all abreast and try to knock the black children off the sidewalk. If they stood their ground, the white children would call the black children names and the black children would call them names back. It never really came to blows, but sometimes it looked as if it would, and Coretta became a little frightened. But being part of a group gave the black children more courage.

In November 1942, Coretta and Edythe found out that their house had burned down. Luckily, no one was hurt. The fire was very suspicious, but the authorities refused to investigate it. The Scotts never found out how the fire started. They had to go and live with Grandfather McMurry.

But Father Scott set an unforgettable example for his family. He simply continued to go to work every day. Soon he had saved up enough money to buy a sawmill. Two weeks after he bought it, a white logger who worked in Scott's mill offered to buy it. Scott said he didn't want to sell. The next Monday when Father Scott went to the sawmill, he found only ashes.

There were a few white people who were friendly toward him, and they advised him to ask for an investigation. But Father Scott knew it was no use, and went back to hauling lumber with his truck for other people, and thinking of other ways to use his skills to set an example for his family. He never became bitter. Watching him, Coretta learned not to hate.

At Lincoln, Coretta learned about many things that were going on in the world, and it was there that her love of music was transformed into a career interest.

All the students at Lincoln had to learn to read music, and anyone who wanted to could study much more. The music teacher at Lincoln was a woman from Pennsylvania named Miss Olive Williams. She had graduated from Howard University, a famous black university in Washington, D.C. Miss Williams taught music appreciation to all students from the seventh grade on. After the students reached the tenth grade, Miss Williams provided private voice instruction. She also played the piano, and gave private piano lessons to those who could afford the small fee. In addition, Miss Williams also directed Lincoln's three choruses. Under her direction, the talented choruses performed complicated works such as *The Messiah* every year for large audiences.

Coretta adored Miss Williams, and it was she who gave Coretta her first formal voice lessons. Soon, Coretta was singing more than ever, performing individually as well as with the Lincoln choruses. At one point, she even took trumpet lessons. She also learned to play the piano, and soon could play quite a few hymns and spirituals.

When Coretta was fifteen, their church asked her to be pianist and choir director, and she even trained the junior choir. In this role, Coretta developed a format for special programs where she would write a narration to go with a spiritual. The narration—about any topic that the song suggested—would be spoken, and then the song would be sung. Many years later, she used this same format for the Freedom Concerts she gave.

While Coretta was studying at Lincoln, she was also keenly observing the faculty. She found something fascinating about these people who worked in the world of academia. There was something special about the black teachers: they were among the black adults in the community who seemed to get the most respect. They had more interesting lives. They traveled to different cities, and they knew more about the world. They knew many different kinds of people, they could talk about many different subjects, and they enjoyed books and music. Although they didn't have very big salaries, they didn't seem always to be worried about money. Coretta concluded it was because they were *educated*. She concluded something else, too: she had to go to college herself.

GOING TO COLLEGE

Coretta had no particular college in mind at first. But it just so happened that music provided a solution. At Lincoln, Coretta's sister Edythe sang in the Lincoln School Little Chorus. This chorus was well known in Marion for its beautiful singing. At that time, two teachers at Lincoln arranged for the Little Chorus to tour various colleges located in other states. One was the all-white Antioch College in Yellow Springs, Ohio. The people there enjoyed the presentation very much.

Two years later, Edythe graduated from Lincoln, and had been such a good student that she was valedictorian of her class. At that same time, Antioch College decided to enroll black students, and to give scholarships to a few of them who could not afford to attend. They remembered the students who had come from Alabama two years before to sing for them, and sent a letter to Lincoln's principal offering a scholarship. Several students applied, and Edythe was awarded a year's scholarship to Antioch, including tuition, room, and board. This was very exciting for Edythe and the whole family. Both she and Coretta wanted to go north, thinking that there they would have more freedom from racial prejudice.

And so it was that in the summer of 1943, Edythe Scott became the very first black student to attend Antioch College on a completely integrated basis. She sent letters to the family regularly, telling of her excitement about Antioch. She told them about how Antioch gave its students a great deal of freedom. There were no housemothers or rules about what time the students had to go to bed. In some exams, certain teachers used the honor system. She wrote about how friendly the white students were. She wrote to Coretta that she would love it there.

Naturally, there were a few negative things that Edythe left out. She did not want to discourage anyone, and she felt the good at Antioch outweighed the bad. It was difficult for Edythe to be the first black person to be admitted to the college. The other students, though friendly enough, thought Edythe would be an authority on race relations, and talked to her about this subject every chance they got. Edythe became very tired of that.

Also, there were other problems, which involved the young men on campus. Some of them enjoyed talking with Edythe because she was intelligent and had many interesting things to say. Edythe was tall and attractive; she had that striking American Indian look of her mother's family. But even if the young men became attracted to her, they didn't have the courage to ask her out. In the three years Edythe was at Antioch, she dated only one white young man, and then only twice. But Edythe didn't mention these things in her letters.

Because of the things Edythe *did* mention in her letters, Coretta could hardly wait to get to Antioch. And she succeeded, too. She had been a very good student, maintaining an A average in her senior year, and was, just as her sister had been, valedictorian of her graduating class. In her senior year, Coretta applied for a partial scholarship to Antioch, and received an award of $450. Her parents had to pay an additional $200 in fees, plus her transportation, but by this time they were able to afford it more easily. Coretta selected Elementary Education as a major.

* * *

Coretta was very excited to be at college. The first thing she noticed was the friendliness of the people she met. There was a strong school spirit at Antioch, and all the students accepted all the other students right away and tried to make them feel at home.

The students at Antioch were predominantly white, and they came from all over the country. There were only six black students in the whole college: in Coretta's freshman class there were Coretta and two others, and in Edythe's class, two besides Edythe.

After Coretta had been there awhile and had more experience, she could sense that under their friendliness, the white students still felt superior because they were white, which Coretta knew had come from generations of hearing myths about black people. They would ask Coretta questions that showed their ignorance, questions Coretta couldn't help resenting, such as "Why are Negroes so boisterous?" Or, "Why are Negroes so immoral?" Or, "Why aren't there more Negro students qualified for Antioch?" But in the South where Coretta came from, whites were not even friendly toward blacks. Instead, they tried to make life difficult for black people and even to harm them physically whenever possible. So Coretta had to admit that at least Antiochians, as the students at Antioch called themselves, tried to overcome their prejudices.

It was not until Coretta's junior year that a white student asked her for a date. He was Jewish, a good musician, and Coretta admired his intelligence. They had a lot in common, and went steady for a year, until he graduated.

The work at Antioch was difficult for Coretta at first. It turned out that her education at Lincoln had not prepared her properly for college. This was not unusual in those days; most of the southern high schools for black students did not expect their graduates to go on to college. So Coretta had to study very hard that first year at Antioch. In her second semester she enrolled in a remedial reading course. She had a lot of catching up to do.

On the whole, Antioch was a very interesting place. The students there did not place a very high value on material things such as clothes. This helped Coretta to manage financially, because she didn't have to spend money on clothes as she might have at other colleges. To Antiochians, the important things were reading books and articles by scholarly authors, and discussing contemporary trends and issues. Coretta did not have any time in her first year to do this kind of outside reading, but later she read a great deal.

Also, the rule at Antioch was for all students to combine their studies with real jobs. As a part of the curriculum, every other semester each student had to hold a real job and to write an evaluation of the job experience. During her Antioch years, Coretta held many such jobs. She worked as a waitress in a dining room; as a camp counselor at a camp that specialized in the arts and music; at a settlement house in one of the worst slum areas in Cleveland; at a nursery school; and as a clerk at several college and public libraries, including a branch of the New York Public Library. One of her jobs was even more fun, and she received college credit for it: she went back home and helped her father in the general store he had opened in 1946.

From all these jobs, Coretta learned how to work with people and for people, in addition to learning the techniques and skills that the job required. It made her studies much more exciting because she could really see how education fit into supporting oneself.

At the time, Coretta was the first black student to major in Elementary Education. Antioch Education majors were required to teach for one year in the Antioch private elementary school, and one year in the Ohio public schools. Coretta chose to teach music, since she had a keen interest in it. The first year, she taught music in the Antioch school. But when she got ready to teach in the public elementary school in the second year, she ran into a problem: although the Yellow Springs schools were integrated, the faculty was all white, and they did not want to have a black teacher in their school system. Coretta was turned down.

The head of the Antioch practice-teaching program was afraid to push the matter because she felt that it might endanger the whole program. So Coretta went to the college president and asked him to appeal to the school board. But he was new to the school, and to make matters worse, he had no courage or sensitivity to race relations. On the teaching supervisor's advice, he refused to do anything about the situation. Coretta was given the choice of either teaching in a segregated black school in another city, or another year at the Antioch school. Not wanting to deal with segregation, Coretta chose to teach at Antioch.

But even though she made the compromise, she was disillusioned and upset. Other teachers and students sympathized with her, and some of them wanted to take action. But nothing helped. Finally Coretta talked herself into action. She said to herself, "Now, I am going to be a Negro the rest of my life, and I have to face these problems. So I'm not going to let this one get me down. I'll have to accept a compromise now, but I don't accept it as being right. I'm going ahead in a more determined way than ever, to do something about this situation. I don't want those who come after me to have to experience the same fate as I did."[3]

And from that time on, Coretta Scott became involved in activities which helped people who were mistreated. Antioch had several groups on campus that were involved in promoting race relations and equal rights: a chapter of the National Association for the Advancement of Colored People (NAACP), a Race Relations Committee, and a Civil Liberties Committee. Coretta joined them all. She also took an interest in promoting world peace, and joined a Quaker peace group. She was determined to do something for all people. She had heard of the words of Horace Mann, the first president of Antioch, who had said in his address to the first graduating class: "Be ashamed to die until you have won some victory for humanity."

STUDYING MUSIC

In addition to teaching music, Coretta also began to study it seriously at Antioch. Music gave her more pleasure than anything else.

The head of the Music Department at Antioch was a black professor named Walter F. Anderson, at that time the college's only black faculty member. Coretta was very impressed by his talent and his knowledge of all kinds of music from classical to jazz. He soon became her second music idol, after Miss Williams at Lincoln High School. Dr. Anderson also became one of the most popular professors at the college.

Dr. Anderson coached Coretta for her first public concert, which was given at the Second Baptist Church in Springfield, Ohio, in 1948. The concert was well received, and was the first of several concerts she presented while she attended Antioch. On one occasion, she had the good fortune to appear on a program with the world-famous black singer Paul Robeson, who encouraged her to continue developing her talent. Her counselors also encouraged her to pursue her musical training at a conservatory of music. Coretta decided that after she got her degree from Antioch, she would attend a music conservatory and specialize in voice in order to develop it to its fullest potential.

But Coretta knew that it would not be a good idea to depend on a career in music as the only means of supporting herself. She had already learned that there were a lot of people who knew music but nothing else, and realized that she would need another skill to fall back on in case something happened to her voice. So she continued to study education, and took courses in other subjects as well, such as economics, chemistry, political science, philosophy, writing, literature, and history.

In 1948 Coretta wrote an essay which appeared in *Opportunity* magazine, published by the Urban League, an organization concerned with securing equal opportunities for black citizens. It was called "Why I Came to College." In it, she told how excited she was about learning. She stated, "The more I work, the easier I find it is to do a good job. A college education has . . . opened a lot of doors leading in a lot of different directions."[4]

When it was time for Coretta to begin applying to music conservatories, Dr. Anderson—who had graduated from Oberlin Conservatory—was very helpful. He made a list of what he considered the five best music conservatories in the country and advised her to apply to them.

In the end, Coretta's choice was between The Juilliard School in New York and the New England

Conservatory of Music in Boston. Coretta was not really excited about living in New York City. Her last job experience as a student had been in New York City, and it had been hard for her to live there. She knew that she would be a struggling student, and was afraid that the impersonal, competitive quality of life in New York might be too much for her. Boston, she assumed, would be easier to adjust to while still about as culturally rich as New York, so she decided to go there. The New England Conservatory of Music accepted her.

Coretta's next task was to obtain financial assistance to help pay her tuition and expenses. With the help of her faculty advisers and counselors, she applied to many foundations and individuals for grants and scholarships. But the closest thing to a favorable reply that she received came from the Jessie Smith Noyes Foundation, which informed her that their grants were already filled for the next year, but if a chosen applicant decided not to use the grant, it would be given to Coretta.

Coretta graduated from Antioch in 1951, with the feeling that her years at the school had been an invaluable preparation for whatever career she chose to follow. Antioch gave her experience in interacting with a community of white people, to learn how they acted and how they thought. This made her realize that she must not expect too much from them, and to make allowances for, without condoning, the inbred beliefs they held.

After graduation, she returned to Alabama to visit her parents. However, she still did not know whether she would be able to afford to go to the New England Conservatory in the fall. Although she knew that her father was able to pay her fees, she felt that she'd been dependent on him long enough, and decided not to ask him for help. She further decided that whether or not she got a scholarship, she would go to Boston. If she didn't get a scholarship, she would just have to get a job, and go to school part-time until she was able to go full-time. She did not even want to take a regular allowance from her parents, but her mother promised to send her a few dollars from time to time.

By the time Coretta was ready to go to Boston, she had still not heard from the Noyes Foundation; she left Alabama with only enough money for her train fare, plus fifteen dollars to cover expenses. When the train stopped in New York, she called home. She was told that a letter had come from the Noyes Foundation, awarding her a grant of $650 to study at the New England Conservatory of Music. Her prayers had been answered!

While attending the conservatory, Coretta planned to board with an Antioch patron named Mrs. Bartol, who rented out rooms to students in her Beacon Hill home. For seven dollars a week, Coretta could have a room and breakfast. Although that was reasonable, Coretta's grant money was just enough to pay her tuition and fees. Coretta realized that she would have to work to earn the money for her board. Still, she decided to enroll full-time at the conservatory.

After a few days in Boston, Coretta had spent most of her fifteen dollars. No money had come from her parents, either. Coretta began to get frightened. She was in trouble, and she didn't know what to do next. How could she get more money? How would she be able to get to school tomorrow?

Suddenly, the phone rang. It was Mrs. Bertha Wormley, a friend of a woman Coretta had met while she had been working in New York. Mrs. Wormley lived in Boston, and had heard that Coretta was studying there. She was calling to ask how Coretta was and if she needed anything. Coretta had never spoken to or met Mrs. Wormley before, but this was her only possible chance to get some money. It was very embarrassing for Coretta to ask Mrs. Wormley for money. But she really had no choice.

Mrs. Wormley did not hesitate one minute. She worked just around the corner from where Coretta lived, and told Coretta to stop by on her way to school.

Coretta was overcome with relief, and rushed over to meet Mrs. Wormley, who handed her an envelope. She did not open it there, but assured the woman that she would pay her back as soon as she could. Mrs. Wormley replied with a smile, "Oh, we'll let our grandchildren worry about it."[5] Coretta left smiling, and went to catch the subway. When it arrived, she sat down and opened the envelope. Inside was fifteen dollars. Coretta began to cry with relief, thinking how lucky she had been to meet someone who was kind enough to help a young woman she hardly knew. Mrs. Wormley never accepted the money back, and Coretta never forgot her kindness.

To be on the safe side, Coretta arranged with Mrs. Bartol to do some work for her so that she could pay for her room. Mrs. Bartol had a very big house, and two other students rented rooms there. She already had a cook and two maids. But she agreed to let Coretta clean up her room, two other bedrooms, the hall, two stairways, and wash the pillowcases and towels on Saturdays. The maids taught Coretta how to scrub the floors the way they did, on hands and knees with sponges and cloths. All this very hard work paid for Coretta's room, her meals, and any extras she needed. In November, however, through the Urban League, she got a part-time job with a mail-order company, and was able to eliminate the Saturday work at Mrs. Bartol's.

The next semester, Coretta got a surprise: a grant from her home state of Alabama. Alabama had a policy of giving grants to black students who wanted to get professional training for which there were no facilities at Alabama's black colleges. But these grants weren't given because the students were talented or financially needy. Instead, they were given to help the students go to other colleges—because the state wanted to keep the Alabama colleges segregated and didn't want the black students at the white colleges! But Coretta was just happy to get the assistance. Later, the conservatory itself awarded her an additional hundred-dollar scholarship, which she applied to her fees.

Three

Courtship and Marriage

Coretta was thrilled to have the opportunity to advance her music studies. All the performances she had previously given and the comments of her teachers and mentors gave her reason to believe that she had enough talent to be successful in a musical career. And being at the New England Conservatory allowed her to develop her musical talents fully. She felt that whether or not she ever worked as a professional musician, she would be a happier person for having taken that opportunity. She had waited so many years, and finally she was in an environment where she was absorbing music.

Most of the students at the conservatory were younger than Coretta, and had just graduated from high school. There were very few black students there—including the students who attended part-time, there were only about fifteen or twenty.

In Boston and other northern cities, there were no WHITES ONLY and COLORED ONLY signs posted, as there were in the South. Still, the black students didn't feel completely welcome at many white restaurants and nightclubs in the Boston area. Because of this, most of the black students' social life took place at parties in private homes, or in one of the restaurants in the area which specialized in southern-style cooking. One such restaurant was called The Western Lunch Box. It was near the conservatory, and black students from the schools in the area often gathered there, although Coretta herself was not able to go there too often because she lived far away.

Coretta kept very busy with her studies and her work. Although she had a deep belief in God, and her family had been religious, churchgoing people, Coretta didn't attend church regularly when she first went to Boston. First of all, she did not feel completely comfortable going to the churches in the all-white Beacon Hill area where she lived, and decided that she could worship in her room instead. Second, she found the religion that she had been brought up in too restrictive and conservative, and had become dissatisfied with organized religion in general. In fact, she was trying to find a church or a faith that was more liberal than the kind she was brought up in and that she would be able to identify with more closely. She made plans to investigate Unitarianism and the Quakers.

MEETING MARTIN LUTHER KING, JR.

One of the conservatory students with whom Coretta became friendly was named Mary Powell. Mary was older than Coretta, and was married to a nephew of Dr. Benjamin Mays, the president of Morehouse College in Atlanta. Coretta was attracted to Mary's intelligence and maturity, and they had a lot in common because they were both from the South. Mary was also somewhat of a matchmaker.

One day in late January 1952, Coretta and Mary were having a chat. Mary said to Coretta, "Have you heard of M. L. King, Jr.?" When Coretta said that she had not, Mary began to tell her about him. "Dr. Mays tells me that he is a very promising young man," she said. "He's a Baptist minister, ordained in his father's church, the Ebenezer Baptist Church in Atlanta. Right now, he's at Boston University taking his doctorate. He has been preaching at churches around Boston and is very brilliant. I want you to meet him."[1]

Mary knew Martin from Atlanta, because when he had attended Morehouse, she had attended Spelman. They met again in Boston, and ate together a lot at The Western Lunch Box. Actually, Martin was almost engaged to a young woman in Atlanta, but he wasn't really enthusiastic about her; it was more of a family assumption that the two would eventually marry because her parents and his were very close. Martin's father wanted him to get married, and offered to help Martin take care of his wife financially until Martin graduated. Although Martin was young, he was extremely mature for his age and he was ready to get married. But he wanted to make his own decisions and to choose his own wife. He knew where he was heading in life and he knew what kind of wife would fit in with that life. So even though there was someone already picked out for him, Martin did not consider his search for a wife ended.

During one of their conversations, Martin told Mary that although he had met quite a few nice young women in Boston, he was beginning to think there were none who would be suitable as a wife for him. "Do you know any nice, attractive young ladies?"[2] he asked her. Mary mentioned two—Coretta and another one. He had already met the other one, so he asked Mary to describe Coretta.

Mary told Martin that Coretta was nice, intelligent, pretty, and so on. But she also let him know that Coretta did not go to church too often, and that she probably was not religious enough. But Martin persuaded Mary to give him Coretta's telephone number anyway.

But now, as soon as Mary mentioned that Martin was a minister, Coretta lost interest. The ministers she had known were too conservative, too righteous, and very narrow-minded, and some of them were hypocrites. And this King was a Baptist, too. Baptists believed that you had to be immersed in water in order to be baptized and have your soul saved. In Coretta's church it was felt that baptism by having the water sprinkled on you was enough. She had heard many discussions among Baptists and non-Baptists about whether it was necessary to be immersed in order to be baptized, and had decided that she would never want to become a Baptist because she didn't feel that baptism by immersion was necessary. So when Mary told her about Martin she dismissed the idea almost immediately.

A few days later, Coretta got a telephone call from Martin. Even though he identified himself, Coretta didn't recognize who he was at first. Then he said, "A mutual friend of ours told me about you and gave me your telephone number. She said some very wonderful things about you and I'd like very much to meet you and talk to you."[3]

Then Coretta began to remember and said, "Oh yes, I've heard some very nice things about you, too."[4] And they began a long conversation. Martin had a strong sense of humor and was smooth but aggressive in his conversation, though very polite. Coretta enjoyed the fun of it. They also talked about each other's studies. Finally Martin said that he'd like to meet her in person, and they arranged to have lunch the next day. Martin promised to pick her up in his car.

The next day was cold and rainy. For her date, Coretta wore a light blue suit and a black coat. Her hair was long, and she had bangs. When Martin's car pulled up, Coretta's first thought when she saw the young man sitting inside was, "How short he seems."[5] (And she was only five feet four inches herself!) And when she got closer, her second thought was, "How unimpressive he looks."[6]

Martin drove to a nearby restaurant, where they had lunch. As Coretta took off her coat, she noticed that Martin was watching her very carefully. She pretended not to notice. He commented that he liked her hair.

As skeptical as Coretta was, after Martin began speaking, it didn't take long for her to realize that there was something very special about him. The strong and convincing way in which he spoke, the language he used, the sincerity of his expression—all of these things were magnetizing to her. He radiated charm, and had a way of attracting people to him from the very first word he spoke. It wasn't very long before Coretta forgot about his height; as he talked, it seemed as if he grew in stature and became better-looking. He carried himself with a very masculine self-possession, and Coretta noticed that he seemed to know exactly where he was going and how he was going to get there. She enjoyed their date very much, and was glad that she had met this young man.

After lunch, Coretta had to go back to her classes.

As they drove back in the car, Martin was very quiet. Suddenly he said to her, "Do you know something?"

"What is that?" Coretta said.

Very quietly but intensely he said, "You have everything I have ever wanted in a wife. There are only four things, and you have them all."

Coretta was caught completely by surprise at this statement. "I don't see how you can say that," she said to him. "You don't even know me."

"Yes, I can tell," Martin continued. "The four things are character, intelligence, personality, and beauty. And you have them all. I want to see you again. When can I?"

At this point it was very difficult for Coretta to maintain her poise. "I don't know," she answered. "I'll have to check my schedule. You may call me later."[7]

All of Coretta's defenses were up. First of all, she did not want anything to stand in the way of her pursuing a career in music. Second, she was no longer a young girl. She had been involved with men before and thought that she was in love, but things had not worked out. She had promised herself that she would not let herself become emotionally involved again until she was absolutely certain. Third, she had not planned to get married for a long time. Although he seemed so serious and sincere, she hoped that Martin had not really meant what he said about marriage. She did like him and wanted to see him again, but not with that kind of pressure.

The next day, Martin called Coretta to ask if she was available on Saturday night. As it happened, Coretta had a tentative date for that night, who was escorting her to a party given by some friends of hers. She told Martin that if the young man could not make it, then Martin could go with her. Martin was agreeable. As it turned out, the other young man was not able to make it, so Martin got a chance to see Coretta a second time.

On the way to the party, Martin and Coretta stopped by the conservatory to see Mary Powell. In front of Coretta, Martin said to her, "Mary, I owe you a thousand dollars for introducing me to this young lady."[8] Coretta smiled.

Martin got quite a lot of attention at the party, especially from the young women. Martin Luther King, Jr., was the most eligible young black man in the Boston area at that time. The women had heard a lot about him, and crowded around him and talked to him. Although he treated Coretta with respect and consideration, he seemed quite pleased with all the attention. Coretta suspected that he was trying to impress her. She was very calm, never letting it appear that it bothered her at all because, of course, she had no claim on him. She never said a word. She just observed.

But some strange, invisible magic happened between them that night, and by the time Martin brought Coretta home, things had moved to a more serious level: Coretta's defenses had come down.

From that day on, Martin assertively pursued Coretta, who did not run from his advances. He loved good conversation, and they spent a great deal of time together and had long, interesting talks about her interests in music and his interests in philosophy. Each was impressed with the extent of the other's knowledge. Often, Martin would talk about the problems black people in America faced, and about how wonderful it could be if they could be free from oppression. But he never thought in terms of gaining that freedom through violence. He believed completely in Christ's words about loving one's enemies.

As Coretta got to know Martin better, she found

him very different from her stereotyped idea of ministers. He was a very good man, with a strong conscience that kept him on the path he thought was right. If he ever did something a little wrong, or committed a selfish act, his conscience would not let him rest. But he was also a fun-loving person whom Coretta found exciting to be with. He loved to tease her, sometimes pretending to like some other young woman until he could see Coretta getting angry. Then he would come over and laughingly console her.

Martin enjoyed parties, and they went to them a lot. He loved to dance, and like Coretta, he loved music. Knowing how much music meant to her, on one of their dates he took her to a concert of classical music at Boston's Symphony Hall, which she could not have afforded to go to on her own. She was grateful that he thought of taking her on that kind of date.

One Sunday, Coretta went to hear Martin preach in a Boston church. She was very impressed with the strength of his words and the powerful way he caught and held the attention of the congregation. She also had a chance to meet Martin's sister, Christine, when Christine visited him in Boston. Christine was also a warm and friendly person, and the two young women got along well. Coretta secretly began to think about marrying Martin.

Martin also told Coretta about the other young woman in Atlanta, and then explained that he preferred to choose his own wife rather than have her be chosen by his parents or anyone else. He again made it clear that Coretta was his choice. He was pleased with the way he and Coretta communicated together, and encouraged her to express her own ideas. Communication, he told her, was a very important ability to him. He also let her know that he believed women are just as intelligent and capable as men and should hold positions of authority and influence.

Coretta discovered, however, that this progressive attitude on Martin's part was combined with more traditional beliefs. For he also made it very clear to Coretta that he would expect whoever he married to be home waiting for him. Even after Coretta had informed Martin that *she* was preparing for a career, he still stated that he wanted his wife to be a homemaker and a mother for his children. Martin was also concerned that Coretta's Antioch experiences and exposures might have caused her to forget her southern roots and the ways of the southern people—the people who would be the members of his congregation, and with whom she would be dealing if she were his wife.

With all of these conflicts, it took Coretta a long time to make a decision about Martin. When she had come to Boston, her studies and her music were the most important things in her life; marriage and a family were the furthest things from her mind. Even if they had not been, she had never in her life even considered marrying a minister. Even with all of Martin's charm, the fun they had together, and the growing closeness between them, she still was not sure.

As the weeks passed, Coretta kept asking herself, "Is this really what I want?" Then she would ask herself, "If I am serious about a commitment to service, how better could I serve than as a minister's wife?"[9] But she was still not convinced that she should marry Martin.

But Martin was working on her, and actually started preparing her for a role as the wife of a Baptist minister. Coretta was not as much of a perfectionist about her appearance as Martin was; in her previous experience, both at home and at Antioch, clothes didn't matter. She had nice clothes but she was not fussy about her appearance. She might comb her hair in the morning and not touch it again all day, or she might not touch up her lipstick.

Martin, on the other hand, was a sharp dresser and was very meticulous about his appearance. He knew that all eyes would be on him, so he dressed with that in mind. Although he, too, believed in not having a lot of material possessions such as clothes, and so on, he did believe in being well-groomed. His hair was always brushed, nails always clean, mustache always trimmed, shoes always polished. So in a very gentle way, Martin would make suggestions to Coretta so that she could be similarly neat. "You look so pretty with lipstick on," he would say. Or he would try to get her to try wearing bright colors that flattered her: "Why don't you buy that pretty red coat we saw in Filene's window?" Or if they were out, he would be always on the alert: "Perhaps you'd like to go to the ladies' room and comb your hair?"[10] Finally, Coretta saw what he was aiming at and began to be more careful about her grooming habits and appearance.

All this time, Coretta was thinking, meditating, concentrating, and praying to be able to make the right decision. By then, she knew that she really loved Martin, and that marriage and a family would make her life more complete. But she would not be able to accept his proposal of marriage until she was satisfied that she could combine the career she loved with being a wife and mother.

It was not until late in the fall of 1952 that Coretta came to a suitable decision that would fit marriage in with the future she wanted for herself. First, she would not leave the conservatory; rather, she would go on and get her degree. This would give her both a credential and a sense of accomplishment, even though she might not do exactly the kinds of work she had planned. Second, she would switch her major from performing arts to musical education and voice, so that instead of having to travel all over the country giving concerts, she would be able to teach wherever they lived.

Once those decisions were made, she decided that she would go ahead and marry Martin, and let the question of her musical career take care of itself.

But she didn't tell Martin right away.

By then, it was summer. Instead of going home to Alabama, Coretta stayed in Boston to study until August, when she was going home to have her tonsils removed. Martin would already be at home in Atlanta, and since she had to pass through Atlanta on her way to Alabama, he asked her to visit him there. This way, she would finally get to meet his parents. But just to test him to see if he really wanted her— and to get him back for so many of the practical jokes he had played on her—she told him she wouldn't. Martin became very upset, and told her that if she didn't want to come she could forget the whole thing. But of course she agreed, and took the train down to Atlanta from Boston. She had arranged to stay with Mary Powell, who was also home for the summer.

When Coretta got off the train, Martin and Mary were there to meet her, and after warm greetings all around, they drove out of the station. After a few blocks, Martin stopped the car and a short, meticulously and fashionably dressed woman got into the car. Martin introduced her to Coretta. The woman was his mother, Mrs. Alberta King! Coretta was very surprised, because she had not expected to meet her so soon. She was already very concerned about how the family would react to her, especially considering that they had already chosen someone for their son to marry. Mrs. King was polite, but casual.

Later, Martin took Coretta to meet his parents officially. They had a very nice house. Martin's father, Martin Luther King, Sr., was a big man, whom everyone called "Daddy King." He was gentle and courteous, but also casual toward Coretta. That night, Coretta stayed at Mary's house.

On Sunday, Coretta went to Ebenezer Baptist Church to hear Martin's sermon. He preached there whenever he was home during the summer, to give his father a rest. He was as stirring as ever, and Coretta felt very proud to see him in his home environment with what would someday probably be his congregation. After the service, Coretta met the rest of Martin's family: his brother Alfred Daniel, whom everyone called A.D.; A.D.'s wife Naomi; and Alveda, their little daughter, who called Coretta "Coco."

The visit went well, and Coretta continued on to Alabama to visit her own parents. She had invited Martin, but he was unable to come. She would later meet him in Atlanta and ride back to school with him and Mary.

In November, Martin's parents were scheduled to visit him in Boston. Martin had told them that Coretta was special, but they didn't seem to take him seriously. So Martin asked Coretta to come by his apartment every afternoon while they were there, so they would get the idea. Soon, they did notice that there seemed to be no other young women in Martin's life; and when he told them that he had decided that Coretta was going to be his wife, they had no choice but to give their blessing. Besides, they liked Coretta anyway, and, when little Alveda had become so attached to her, they knew she had to be a good person!

After Martin's parents left, Coretta and Martin

began to discuss marriage seriously. Coretta finally let him know that she would marry him, and they decided to get married in June, after the school year ended.

MARRIAGE

Martin and Coretta were married by Daddy King on June 18, 1953. The wedding took place on the lawn of Coretta's parents' new home, recently built by Father Scott next door to his general store. The King and Scott families met for the first time that day.

Coretta had decided that she didn't want to have a typical wedding. She still had that Antioch dislike of material things, and she didn't want to wear a formal white gown. Neither did she bother with the traditional bridal custom of choosing patterns for silver or china. At her and Martin's request, the section of the marriage vows where the bride promises to obey was omitted. And Coretta cooked part of the wedding dinner herself.

The wedding was a private affair, and Coretta wore a pale blue, waltz-length gown with matching shoes and gloves. It was a big, lovely wedding, with 350 guests: the whole King family, some of whom had traveled great distances to attend, the trustees of Ebenezer, and friends.

After the reception, Martin and Coretta went to Marion. But they were both tired: Coretta, because she had been involved in all the wedding preparations, and Martin because he had driven all the way from Boston. Martin was so tired he slept all the way to Marion.

In those days, there were very few hotels that accepted black guests, and none with bridal suites; black married couples frequently had to stay in the homes of friends. The Kings' wedding night was spent at the home of friends who were undertakers. Later, they often joked about that.

On the Sunday following their wedding, Martin preached at Ebenezer. He introduced Coretta to the congregation, and she joined the church and was baptized by immersion. The next day, she went to work as a clerk in the Atlanta Citizens' Trust Company, a bank of which Daddy King was a director. Since they planned to return to school in Boston in the fall, they lived in Martin's parents' house all summer.

Four

Early Years with Martin Luther King, Jr.

Married life for Coretta began pretty much as she had expected. They took an apartment in Boston near Martin's old one, and shared equally in the household duties. They continued their respective studies, and were both very, very busy: Martin was working on his doctoral dissertation and occasionally preaching at churches in Boston. Coretta was in her final year. She had to study choir directing, orchestral arrangement and directing, piano, and voice, as well as take classes in brass, percussion, strings, and woodwinds, so that she would be able to teach those subjects. She also had to do practice teaching at one high school and two elementary schools.

That first year of their marriage was the calmest period of their entire married life. After that, life would never be calm again.

In March 1954, Martin was invited to become the pastor of the Dexter Avenue Baptist Church in Montgomery, Alabama. He wasn't sure how to respond to the invitation, because he and Coretta were enjoying their quiet life in the North. Besides, Coretta wanted to stay and pursue a career in music. But on May 17, 1954, the United States Supreme Court decided the case of *Brown v. Board of Education of Topeka, Kansas*, ruling that segregation in public schools was unconstitutional. Martin sensed that this would be the beginning of important changes for black people, so he decided that he wanted to be in the South to help. Coretta agreed, and Martin accepted the invitation.

On the first Sunday in July 1954, Martin took Coretta with him to the Dexter Avenue Baptist Church to meet his new congregation. He had told her that he would ask her to speak, and she had prepared a speech and memorized it. Before the service began, Martin introduced Coretta to the congregation and announced that she would say a few words.

Coretta smiled and spoke to the members, thanking them for inviting Martin to be their pastor, and telling them that she looked forward to living in their community and working with them. She added that this would be a new experience for her and asked for their prayers to help her to become a good minister's wife. But privately, she was concerned that she would not be that useful to the church. She didn't want to be an important leader or anything like that, but she did want to feel as if she were a part of things.

When she met the members after the service, they told her that they were looking forward to the Kings' move there in September. The Kings were then taken to see the parsonage, the house where the pastor and his family were to live. It was a white wooden house, nice but rather run-down, located in a segregated neighborhood almost a mile from the church. It had a porch and seven large rooms. The church members promised that they would furnish and redecorate the house in whatever way the Kings liked.

After meeting the church members and seeing the church and the house, Coretta felt more comfortable. She was getting the feeling that it was going to be a place where maybe she could be useful, although she had no idea of just how. She told Martin, "If this is what you want, I'll make myself happy here. You will perfect your preaching and improve yourself in the ministry at Dexter, and I will learn to be a good minister's wife."[1]

In September 1954, Coretta and Martin moved into the parsonage. Even though it was just the two of them, they were very busy. Martin would get up at 5:30 every morning to work on his dissertation for three hours. After dinner he worked on it for three more hours. During the day he took care of church matters such as committee meetings, performing marriages, conducting funerals, and visiting each of the three hundred members of the church. The Kings also spent time with another young black minister in Montgomery named Ralph Abernathy, and his wife, Juanita. The Abernathys were also very strongly committed to social reform, and before Martin had accepted the invitation to preach at Dexter, he had sought Abernathy's advice on being a young black minister in that southern city.

Martin also spent fifteen hours a week preparing his sermons. He would start by writing out the sermon on Tuesday. He would discuss his ideas with Coretta and ask for her suggestions, which he sometimes incorporated into the sermons. By Saturday night, he had memorized it; and on Sunday morning the congregation was always very impressed that he could speak spontaneously for forty minutes. In church, Coretta would listen and let Martin know afterward how he had sounded. She also observed the congregation and reported their reactions. Martin frequently stated that Coretta was his best critic.

Coretta was also useful in other ways. She acted as Martin's secretary and worked on various church committees. And because she was the only member who had extensive musical training, she helped as much as she could to make Dexter's choir the best in Montgomery. She sang in the choir, often performing solo parts of anthems or oratorios. She was also frequently asked to perform concerts in other cities. And in addition to all these activities, Coretta had to cook, clean, and keep house.

In October they took two weeks off to go to Boston so that Martin could write the first draft of his dissertation. Coretta remained in their hotel room day and night, retyping it—it was almost 350 pages long!

The spring of 1955 was a very special one: Martin received his Ph.D. in theology, and Coretta discovered that she was pregnant. They were both excited and happy. Martin wanted a son so that he could name him Martin Luther King III, but the baby, born on November 17, 1955, was a girl. Martin was not at all disappointed. They named her Yolanda, and called her Yoki for short. Their lives were complete.

But less than three weeks later, just as they were getting used to the experience of being parents, something happened that changed their lives—and the lives of black people all over the country—forever.

THE MOVEMENT BEGINS

One of the facts of everyday life in the South was segregated buses: it was a law that white people rode in the front of the buses, and black people rode in the back. The buses had little signs reading WHITE FORWARD, COLORED REAR. If all of the WHITE seats were filled and more white people got on, the seated black people were asked to get up and give the white people their seats.

On December 1, 1955, a black woman named Rosa Parks was sitting on a bus in Montgomery. She had worked hard all day and was tired. All of the WHITE seats were filled, and when more white people got on, Mrs. Parks was asked to give up her seat. She refused. A policeman was called, and when he asked her to stand, she replied, "I don't think I should have to stand. Why do you push us around?" The policeman said, "I don't know, but the law is the law, and you're under arrest."[2]

Mrs. Parks's arrest interested Mr. E. D. Nixon, a black community leader for whom Mrs. Parks had worked as a secretary. He asked her if he could use her case to try to bring an end to segregation on the buses in Montgomery, and she agreed.

Mr. Nixon contacted all the black ministers and community leaders in the city to arrange for a meeting to plan a strategy. When Martin was called, even though he knew nothing yet about the situation, he offered the Dexter Avenue Baptist Church as a meeting place. Coretta, still recuperating from childbirth, could not be present at the meeting.

At the meeting, the leaders, realizing that a unified protest would bring greater results, decided that the black people should stay off the buses for one day—a "boycott."

There were about fifty thousand black people in the city of Montgomery. The leaders informed them all of the plan through the many community organizations and churches. Everybody spread the word and helped out. Thirty-five thousand notices were typed, printed, and distributed by a teacher named

Jo Ann Robinson at Alabama State College and some of her students. The notices read:

> *Another Negro woman has been arrested and thrown into jail because she refused to get up out of her seat on the bus for a white person to sit down. Please, children and grown-ups, don't ride the bus at all on Monday. Please stay off all buses Monday.*

Within two days, all fifty thousand black people knew of the boycott plan. On Sunday, the day before the boycott, Coretta and Martin were up most of the night answering the many calls that came and talking about how the boycott might turn out. They both doubted that it would be successful, but Coretta found herself impressed by the role the women of the community were playing in all of this.

At 5:30 the next morning, they got up and stood at the window to watch the buses roll by. They were amazed and pleased to see that on December 5, 1955, not one black person rode on a Montgomery bus.

That night, there was a meeting in a Montgomery church. Martin, whose style was by now earning him praise, was invited to be one of the speakers. The black people were so proud that they had made an effective show of solidarity that they voted unanimously to continue the boycott. The time was right: black people had been mistreated for so long and in so many ways, and they were tired.

The community leaders decided to form an association, which they named the Montgomery Improvement Association, to plan the strategies for the boycott. To his surprise, Martin, still new in town, was elected president of the association because he was new and young, with a strong voice and a rational mind. He accepted the position, and instead of suggesting that they go out and fight, he guided them to use the "weapon of protest," nonviolent resistance. This was one of the principles taught by the Indian leader Mohandas K. Gandhi, and by following it, a whole country had been led to independence. Martin had studied Gandhi's teachings, and sensed that they would be perfect to use in the Montgomery situation.

From that day on, the black citizens of Montgomery walked or used the system of car pools that they created for the purpose. They walked in the rain, the heat, and the cold. They had meetings in the church to discuss strategy and to be encouraged. Martin continued to lead the people and guide them with his strength.

When the Montgomery Improvement Association was formed, the King home served as its office. Even though Coretta was just getting used to being a mother, she quickly got caught up in the excitement of the circumstances and began to help in whatever way she could to make things move more smoothly. The other women in the community offered help, too, and they were always ready to provide support and company.

From the very beginning, the Kings' privacy was completely gone. All day long, the house was always full, with groups of people meeting throughout the house. The phone would ring from 5:00 A.M. until midnight. There were reporters who waited at the house until Martin could get home. They and other visitors—and most of the time Coretta never knew exactly how many—had to be fed. Coretta learned to cook large quantities of food and to get used to the fact that it would rarely be eaten at the moment it was ready, but might sit on top of the stove for hours. For example, Martin might leave a meeting and bring all the participants home to eat with him! Coretta also quickly realized that it would be impossible to keep Yoki on any sort of schedule, so instead of worrying about it, she decided the baby would have to learn to adapt with the rest of them. And whenever Martin traveled, he always left Coretta at home because he thought it made people feel better just to see her, and he knew that she would attend the meetings he was unable to attend.

At first, the black people only wanted the system of segregation on the buses to be fairer than it already was, and they tried to negotiate with the white authorities. But the whites refused to listen to the black people, and would not cooperate. So since the black people had nothing more to lose, they decided that they might as well try to stop the buses from being segregated at all. They voted not to return to the buses until that goal was attained.

The leaders decided to file a lawsuit in federal court which alleged that segregation on buses was unconstitutional. The white people tried to retaliate by arresting the black leaders under an old anti-boycott law, but it didn't work: the protest continued. By now the national newspapers and radio and television stations were becoming interested, and writers and photographers recorded what they saw and exposed it to the rest of the country. What they saw included Martin, and his face soon became a familiar one on television and in newspapers and magazines.

As the boycott went on, organizations and churches from all over the country began to invite Martin to speak at their gatherings. He accepted many of these invitations in order to raise money the movement needed. As the events in Montgomery became publicized, the Kings had many visitors from all over the country and the world who came to meet Martin and offer their assistance to the cause.

The boycott hurt businesses in Montgomery, not to mention the bus company. In the meantime, the cities of Richmond, Virginia; Little Rock, Arkansas; and Dallas, Texas, had ended segregation on their buses, which only made Montgomery, Alabama, look worse.

When the white city officials in Montgomery realized that the blacks were serious, they started a policy to retaliate and to wear the blacks down. They arrested black citizens on the most petty of charges. It wasn't long before Martin realized that this could happen to him, too, and tried his best to avoid being arrested. But Coretta commented that if he *were* arrested, it would be a good thing because it would make the people angry and unite them even more, and embarrass the city officials at the same time. Martin agreed, and sure enough the next time he was driving downtown, very carefully, he was stopped by a policeman. When the policeman found out who he was, Martin was accused of speeding and taken to jail. The news spread, and soon there were so many protesters that the police released Martin.

But the harassment continued. The Kings received many threatening telephone calls. They discussed what they would do in case anything happened. One of the things they considered was that their house might be bombed, even though the house was located in a densely populated area in the heart of the city. Because the front of the house was the most accessible, since it was directly on the street, they decided to move the sleeping quarters to the back of the house, which had a deep yard with a fence around it. No one could get too close to the back.

In spite of all the work, confusion, danger, and

the chaos of their private lives, Coretta felt inspired. She was very excited to be a part of what looked like a bigger movement, maybe even a nationwide movement, which was being born right before their eyes. And she was right: it was the beginning of a people's protest against the denial of their rights. It was the beginning of the Civil Rights Movement.

THE KINGS ARE ATTACKED

On Monday, January 30, 1956, Coretta and Yoki were alone in the house with a friend of Coretta's. Martin was away at a meeting. Around nine-thirty in the evening, Coretta was in the living room and heard something heavy drop on the floor of the porch. Instead of running toward the sound, Coretta grabbed the baby and they all ran to the back of the house. As they did, there was a loud explosion on the porch which shook the whole house. The windows all broke and the porch split in two, but fortunately, none of them was hurt. The incident was reported in the national news.

Although Coretta was brave about it, she began to realize the danger of their situation. But after considering the importance of the cause, both she and Martin accepted that they had no choice but to continue. Too many people were beginning to look up to Martin as a leader and to Coretta as a brave, organized helper who gave him the moral support to continue the leadership. So they decided to stay. After the house was repaired, a friend stayed there as a bodyguard, and they hired a watchman and a babysitter and installed floodlights around the house. They refused, however, to keep weapons or to have armed security.

Finally, on November 13, 1956, the United States Supreme Court upheld the Alabama state court's earlier ruling that the Montgomery bus segregation was unconstitutional. A vote was taken and the black people voted to call off the boycott. It had been intended for one day, but had lasted for eleven months and eight days!

ONSTAGE IN NEW YORK

Even though the boycott was over, the Montgomery Improvement Association stayed intact. A number of the black political and professional leaders who were becoming involved with the civil rights movement had planned a big concert at Manhattan Center in New York on December 5, 1956 (the first anniversary of the boycott), to raise money for the association. Stars like Duke Ellington and Harry Belafonte were to perform. And among these great stars, Coretta was the featured performer.

Manhattan Center was completely full that night. Coretta looked very glamorous in a strapless gown trimmed in white at the top. In her part of the program, she was accompanied by a pianist. First she sang several classical pieces. Then she told the story of the Montgomery bus boycott in both words and song. She used the format she had invented in Lincoln High School: she told the story of the Movement and wove the spirituals and the freedom songs into the narration.

Coretta spoke briefly of the oppression suffered through the ages by many people and how God had always sent deliverers to them. She mentioned that it had been a year ago on that day that the struggle to end economic, political, and social injustice began, and for almost one year, black people in Montgomery walked in dignity rather than ride in humiliation. Then she sang one of the spirituals the people sang to give them moral support as they walked to and from their jobs. She spoke of the strength of the women, telling the story of the old woman who, walking during the boycott just like the rest, had said, "It used to be that my soul was tired, while my feets rested. Now my feets' tired, but my soul is resting."[3] She spoke of the threats and violence they had all endured, and their determination to keep on in spite of them. After each narration, she would sing a spiritual, such as "Let My People Go," that illustrated the narration.

Her words showed the commitment that she had made to the struggle: "We are determined that there shall be a new Montgomery, a new Southland, yes, a new America, where freedom, justice, and equality shall become a reality for every man, woman, and child. We have felt all along in our struggle that we have cosmic companionship—that God Himself is on our side—and that truth and goodness ultimately will triumph. This is our faith, and by this faith we shall continue to live."[4]

At the end of the program she sang "Honor, Honor," one of Martin's favorite spirituals.

It was at this performance that Coretta first met the singer Harry Belafonte, who was to become one of the Kings' closest friends. From that point on, whenever there was trouble or tragedy, Harry Belafonte was always one of the first people to come to their assistance.

The Supreme Court decision gladdened the black people but angered the whites, who continued to commit acts of violence toward blacks. There were many unsolved bombings in Montgomery. As a result, Martin and several black leaders thought it would be a good idea to establish an umbrella group for support and solidarity reasons, which would include all the black leaders throughout the South. Coretta and Martin hosted several meetings of the

Montgomery leaders in their home, and they planned the agenda for a meeting of the leaders from other states. The meeting was scheduled to be held at Ebenezer Baptist Church in Atlanta on January 10–11, 1957, but the continuing violence in Montgomery required that Martin be there to calm the people. Martin asked Coretta to represent him at the meeting of the leaders.

Coretta was the first speaker. She explained why Martin could not be present, and gave the news of the violence in Montgomery. She presented the agenda to the group and a vote was taken to accept it. Then the meeting began and the speakers spoke. As a result of this meeting, the Southern Christian Leadership Conference, or SCLC, was born. Again, the organization operated out of the King home, and Coretta continued to assist.

A VISIT TO AFRICA

By 1957, the Kings had become more popular, important, and visible. Leaders around the world were watching what was happening with the black people's struggle for equality in the South.

Across the globe, another black people's struggle for freedom had been won: the African country of Ghana (previously called the Gold Coast) had just won its independence from Great Britain. Blacks in America—particularly blacks in the South—were very encouraged by this event. Coretta and Martin were pleased and moved when they received an invitation from Kwame Nkrumah, the head of the new government of independent Ghana, to be present at the Independence Day ceremonies in Accra, the capital of Ghana.

They could not afford the trip, however, and knew they would have to decline the invitation. But the whole community was excited because it would be Martin and Coretta's first trip outside of the United States, and they wanted them to have the experience. They also felt a strong sense of identification with the African people's struggle. So they took up a collection. The members of Dexter Avenue Baptist Church collected $2,500, and the Montgomery Improvement Association gave another $1,000 toward the trip.

And so it was that on March 3, 1957, Martin and Coretta left for Africa. Attending the ceremony were representatives of sixty-eight nations, among them Vice President Richard Nixon, who represented the United States. There was much pomp and ceremony during the several days they were there. The most memorable moment for Coretta and Martin came at midnight on March 6, when the British flag was lowered and the new flag of Ghana was raised.

Coretta and Martin made the most of their trip: the next day, they flew to Nigeria for a quick tour. They were amazed at the poverty of the people. Then they traveled to Rome, where they visited the Vatican, then Geneva, Paris, and London.

When they returned, the NAACP awarded Martin the Spingarn Medal, which is an award given to the person who made the greatest contribution to race relations in the previous year. Coretta was proud and pleased. And she was even more proud and pleased when she discovered that she was pregnant again.

By then, the Kings were national figures and in great demand. Martin was deluged with requests from all over the world to appear and give speeches. From 1957 to 1958 Coretta hardly saw Martin! He delivered over two hundred speeches and traveled over 750,000 miles. He also wrote *Stride Toward Freedom,* a book in which he described the Montgomery bus boycott. At one point, he had to hide out in the home of friends until his manuscript was finished.

The Kings' second child, a boy, was born on October 23, 1957. They named him Martin Luther King III. Coretta was somewhat ambivalent about naming the child after his father; she felt that it might be a problem for him in the future, since his father was so famous. But Coretta agreed because it was so important to Martin.

The following summer, Coretta and Martin finally got a chance to take their first real vacation since their marriage: they went to Mexico for two weeks. They made sure they were not disturbed; Martin made no speeches and they conducted no business.

When they returned from this vacation, it was business as usual. This meant more white harassment. On one occasion, when Martin was attending a hearing at which Ralph Abernathy was testifying, a court officer told him to "move along" in the hall. Martin refused, and was arrested. He was taken to the police station, and released on his own recognizance. This experience gave him an idea: if he would actually be jailed, there would be more embarrassment and accountability for the white authorities. Thus, he told Coretta that he would no longer accept bail, and that next time he was arrested he would serve the time.

In September 1958, *Stride Toward Freedom,* dedicated to Coretta, was published. The book received excellent reviews, and the publisher arranged for Martin to go on a national tour to promote it. One of the tour stops was New York City, where Martin spent some time in Blumstein's, a Harlem department store, autographing copies of the book. Suddenly, a woman came up to him and asked if he was

Martin Luther King. When he said that he was, she pulled out a very sharp letter opener and stabbed him in the chest.

Martin did not lose consciousness, and remained calm and motionless until an ambulance arrived. He was taken to the hospital and operated on to remove the letter opener—which was just one inch from his heart. Fortunately, he was expected to recover.

When Coretta heard the news, she rushed to New York to be with him. Concealing her worry, she took charge of the situation, just as she did at home. There were hundreds of people who wanted to visit him in the hospital. Thousands of people sent letters, telegrams, flowers, and baskets of fruit. It became Coretta's job to screen visitors to decide which ones would be allowed to see him, to see that the surplus flowers and fruit were put to good use, and that the letters and telegrams were answered.

Martin soon recovered, and in March of the following year he decided that it was the right time to accept a previous invitation to visit Prime Minister Jawaharlal Nehru in India. Martin had long wanted to visit that country, because the Indian people's struggle for independence had many things in common with the black people's struggle for civil rights in America. India, like Ghana, was a country whose people had gained independence from Great Britain.

Coretta accompanied Martin on this trip in March of 1959. She was also present when Martin and Nehru met at the prime minister's home. They talked about Gandhi and the future of the Indian people for about four hours. Coretta was quiet most of the time, listening.

During the next few days, they traveled throughout the country, because Martin had speeches to make. Most of the time, after Martin made his speech, Coretta gave a performance of spirituals,

Coretta Scott, one of the first black students admitted to Antioch College, is pictured here during her Antioch years.

The Reverend and Mrs. King stand in front of a group of cheering supporters after King was convicted for his role in the Montgomery bus boycott. He was fined $500.

Coretta, Yolanda, and Martin Luther III greet Martin Luther King, Jr., after the reverend's release from Reidsville Prison under a $2,000 appeal bond in October 1960.

Coretta and Dr. King (holding hands, center right) lead approximately ten thousand marchers on the last leg of their Selma-to-Montgomery civil rights walk, March 25, 1965.

The King family sings freedom songs to celebrate the news that Martin Luther King, Jr., had been awarded the Nobel Peace Prize. Reverend King was in a local hospital for a rest and checkup when the prize was announced in October 1964.

The Reverend and Mrs. Martin Luther King, Sr., Coretta Scott King, and Mrs. Christine Farris (Dr. King's sister) are ready to board a plane from New York's John F. Kennedy airport, to meet Dr. Martin Luther King, Jr., in London. The next stop is Oslo for the presentation of the Nobel Peace Prize!

Coretta, her children, and friends gather around the coffin of Martin Luther King, Jr.

*Coretta listens gravely at her husband's
funeral, surrounded by friends.*

The Ebenezer church would always be a special part of the King family's memories.

Coretta Scott King addresses a Peace-in-Vietnam Rally in New York City's Central Park, April 27, 1968. Although her husband was killed only a few weeks earlier, Coretta Scott King would continue his work and fight for peace and civil rights for all.

Coretta Scott King talks with Prime Minister Hugh Shearer of Jamaica, after accepting the Marcus Garvey Prize for Human Rights that was awarded to Dr. King posthumously by the Jamaican government.

Coretta Scott King presented the Emmys to the winners of the television "News Awards" at the June, 8, 1969 ceremony. One of the awards was for outstanding television coverage of Dr. King's assassination.

On November 2, 1983, President Reagan signs a bill establishing a legal holiday in honor of Martin Luther King, Jr. Coretta Scott King watches as the honor she worked for so diligently becomes a reality.

At the 1984 Democratic National Convention, Coretta Scott King speaks on civil rights. Her son Dexter stands behind her.

Bernice, Coretta, and Martin Luther III, were arrested June 26, 1985, for protesting against apartheid at the South African Embassy in Washington, D.C.

On June 27, 1990, South African leader Nelson Mandela (second from left) visits the Martin Luther King memorial at the King Center in Atlanta. Coretta Scott King is third from the left.

which the Indian people loved. As they traveled and met the people, Coretta found that women played a very big part in the political life of India, and she was very impressed by this. Women were much more involved in India than they were in the United States: Gandhi had involved the women of India in the struggle for independence, and many of them had gone to jail like the men. Gandhi had also worked to liberate women from the bondage of Hindu and Muslim traditions. After learning these things, Coretta thought that if she had known, before meeting with the prime minister, how much progress the women of India had made with the coming of independence, she would have made some comments on that topic.

All in all, it was a trip Coretta never forgot. From seeing the strength of the women around her, she had long been convinced that the women of the world, united without any regard for national or racial divisions, could become a powerful force for international peace and brotherhood. She promised herself that she would increase her activities in women's organizations that addressed social issues, such as the Women's International League for Peace and Freedom.

MOVING TO ATLANTA

The following year, Coretta and Martin had a decision to make. The demands on Martin's time were increasing: speaking and traveling all over the country as well as all over the world, being a public figure, the events taking place in the Civil Rights Movement, being the president of the SCLC and traveling back and forth to its Atlanta offices, all meant that his attention was taken away from his duties as pastor at Dexter. So after discussing it with Coretta, Martin decided that the best thing for him to do would be to resign from the Dexter pastorship. At the end of January 1960, the family moved to Atlanta to focus on the work of the SCLC and the Movement. Martin decided to be copastor with his father at Ebenezer; there would be less pressure, and it would give him time to work at his other projects.

After the Kings moved to Atlanta, the SCLC began to grow. Soon, it outgrew the space in their home and the staff moved to larger office quarters. Coretta was not needed for the duties she had previously performed, such as reading and answering all the mail they received. Instead, she turned her attention to saving as much material as she could—records, press releases, speeches—for the children and for the record. She knew that these things would someday have historical value.

Soon after the Kings arrived in Atlanta, Martin was indicted on a charge of falsifying his income tax returns. It was suggested that he had received money from the Montgomery Improvement Association and from the SCLC, and this money had not been reported to the state.

Because Martin was a very thorough record-keeper and Coretta was extremely organized, they both knew that this charge was absolutely false, and was part of the now regular harassment of Martin and his family. But Martin was still very upset about the charge. He felt that people who didn't know him might believe it. The community, as usual, supported him and contributed to his defense. During the subsequent trial, Coretta spent many long days in court, but she was confident that justice would prevail. And so it did: in May of 1960, Martin was acquitted of the charges. But the experience had angered them both.

The night of the verdict, Coretta was scheduled to

travel to Cleveland, Ohio, with Ralph Abernathy to speak at three services for the Antioch Baptist Church Women's Day. She was still very wound up from the events of the trial, and when they arrived at Antioch at 5:00 A.M., she still had not finished writing her speech. She could not decide whether to use the written speech or simply to talk, without notes, about some of the things that had happened to her recently. Abernathy suggested that she talk about her experiences that week at Martin's trial. And that is what she did: after being introduced to the congregation, the words poured out and Coretta spoke for forty minutes.

The violence toward blacks in the South was increasing. But so were the newspaper, magazine, and television reports filed by the many reporters present. In fact, media coverage became one of the most important factors in the Civil Rights Movement. The media attention to the cruelty taking place in the South caused people around the country and around the world to become aware of what was happening there—events that perhaps no one would have believed had they not seen them happening. Today, those black-and-white photographs and films may seem crude and unreal in comparison to the sophisticated technological marvels now available. But in the 1950s television was a new thing, and television cameras were heavy, large pieces of equipment. Yet the events that were captured with them have become a major part of history and we are fortunate to be able to see them. Gradually, the publicity gave black people confidence that the eyes of the nation and perhaps the world were on the South.

Yet another unpleasant fact of segregated life for blacks in the South was at restaurants and lunch counters. In those days, blacks could only be served at counters which had signs reading COLORED ONLY. The success of the bus boycott had made the blacks more determined to break down segregation wherever it existed, and restaurants and lunch counters were the next target.

On February 1, 1960, in Greensboro, North Carolina, four black college students decided to go and sit at a lunch counter in Woolworth's and wait until they were served. They knew that it was dangerous and could result in their going to jail, but they were brave young men. They acted with respect, spoke properly, and were well dressed. They went to the lunch counter and ordered coffee. The waitress said, "I'm sorry, but we don't serve colored here."

They were ignored, and were not served, but there was no incident. Soon, black leaders caught on to the idea and began to organize these protests, which were called "sit-ins," every day at lunch counters throughout the city. They were determined to do this until segregation was defeated. As time went on, violence against the students began, and the students—but not the whites who attacked them—were arrested. But whenever the students were arrested or beaten, the next day more students sat in at more segregated lunch counters. Students all over the country began to do the same.

Martin was impressed that students were taking on the brave responsibility of protesting. The older people had suffered long enough, and Martin realized that young people could be the strongest forces in the Movement; they were seeing terrible things happen to their elders and asking, "What can I do?" They respected their elders and their families, they were well behaved, and they were energetic and brave. So Martin decided to help organize the youngsters and form the Student Non-Violent Coordinating Committee, or SNCC. The goals of SNCC were to desegregate public lunch counters, rest rooms, parks, theaters, and schools; to register all blacks in the South to vote; and to get whites to practice non-discriminatory practices in hiring. Martin joined some of these protests, and just as he and Coretta had discussed, he was arrested and jailed.

By this time Yoki was almost five and Marty was almost three, and Coretta was again pregnant. She was at least as busy as Martin: she had to fulfill speaking and singing engagements, assist Martin, and raise two small children. At this point, the children were old enough to realize their daddy was famous, and were getting used to hearing his name on the radio and seeing his face on television. Coretta knew that one day she would have to explain his work to them, and tried to prepare herself for it in advance.

The day came. As they were being driven home from nursery school, the children heard the news on the radio that Martin had been arrested. Yoki came home crying and both she and Marty asked Coretta, "Why did Daddy go to jail?"

Coretta was ready. "Your daddy is a brave and kind man," she explained. "He went to jail to help people. Some people don't have enough to eat, or comfortable homes, or enough clothing to wear. Daddy went to jail to make it possible for all people to have these things. Don't worry, your daddy will be coming back."[5]

Somewhat later, Coretta found out how effective her explanation had been. She was told of a conversation between Yoki and a little white girl who was one of her classmates. The girl said in a derogatory tone, "Your daddy is always going to jail." Yoki replied calmly and proudly, "Yes, he goes to jail to help people."[6] And that was the end of that.

When Martin went to jail, part of Coretta would be imprisoned with him. But as deeply involved in the Movement as Coretta already was, she wanted to prove the extent of her commitment by participating in the activities that might lead to being arrested. She strongly realized the value of the public seeing innocent people being arrested and jailed, and felt that if she could also be jailed it would have a great effect. She sometimes felt that her participation was not complete because she did not have this experience. But Martin never wanted her to risk being jailed while the children were so young.

This time, Martin was sentenced, because of a previous traffic violation, to six months of hard labor. Coretta was now five months' pregnant, and the harsh sentence took her by surprise. She was very upset and shocked, and for the first time since the Movement began in 1955, she cried in public when she heard the verdict.

Coretta visited Martin every day, but after the eighth day, she was pretty worn out from anxiety and the daily trips. She was also feeling sorry for herself, thinking that such a long sentence meant that he would still be in jail when the baby arrived, and she would have to have the baby without him. Because of all these thoughts, she could not help crying when she went to visit him. He was used to the strong Coretta, the Coretta who kept things organized and kept a happy and warm home for him so that he could do his work in comfort. Seeing her this way surprised him. "You have to be strong for me," he reminded her.

Suddenly, without warning, that night Martin was taken in chains and handcuffs to a solitary cell in a jail three hundred miles away. When Coretta found out, she felt frustrated and very helpless. And of course, she was not able to visit him as often since it took a whole day to make the round trip.

One day soon afterward, as Coretta was getting dressed to go and visit an attorney with Daddy King, she received a telephone call. It was from Senator John F. Kennedy, who was in the final days of his presidential campaign. He said, "I want to express to you my concern about your husband—I know this must be very hard for you. I understand you are expecting a baby, and I just wanted you to know that I was thinking about you and Dr. King. If there is anything I can do to help, please feel free to call on me."[7]

Coretta was grateful to hear Senator Kennedy's concern, but she was not quite sure how to react. She realized that the phone call could be used to political advantage, but Martin had a policy of not endorsing political candidates. Coretta did not want to get either herself or Martin identified with either political party.

She was very diplomatic when she replied. "I certainly appreciate your concern," Coretta said. "I would appreciate anything you could do to help."[8]

After that telephone call, things began to happen fast. Coretta began to hear some encouraging reports about Martin's release. She heard that Robert Kennedy, Senator Kennedy's brother and campaign manager, who was an attorney, called the judge to learn why Martin couldn't be released on bail pending appeal. The story of that call, too, leaked out to the press, and the judge, embarrassed, changed his mind and said that Martin would be released on bail. Martin came home the next day. The whole family was ecstatic with joy.

The night Martin returned, there was a welcoming meeting at Ebenezer. True to his policies, Martin said nothing political. But Daddy King, who had been planning to vote for Nixon, roared out to the crowd, "If I had a suitcase full of votes, I'd take them all and place them at John F. Kennedy's feet!"[9] A few days later, the election took place, and John F. Kennedy was elected president by only about 100,000 votes. Many people believed that his intervention in Martin's case won him the presidency.

Coretta's baby, a boy, was born on January 30, 1961. The baby was named Dexter Scott, after the church in which Martin had preached.

The sit-ins continued, and the members of SNCC also launched a protest against segregated interstate buses. In the same way that they had decided to disobey the segregation rules at lunch counters, they decided that they would get on the interstate bus lines and bring attention to the bus policy of segregation. They called these "trips" Freedom Rides, and they promised to keep doing it "till we can ride from anywhere in the South to anywhere else in the South without comment." Whites who were sympathetic to the civil rights cause were asked to join these rides, and they began in May 1961. Arrests and violence were everyday occurrences, but still the black people did not use violence themselves. They wanted to make sure the world saw the oppression that the whites were subjecting them to.

As these events were taking place, both Martin and Coretta were rushing around the country to gain moral and financial support for the Movement. Martin was making speeches, and Coretta was also making speeches and giving concerts.

APPEALING FOR PEACE

In late March of 1962, Coretta received a very special invitation. By then it was well known that she took an active interest in promoting world peace. Because of this, she was invited by a women's group, the Women's Strike for Peace, to travel to Geneva, Switzerland, to participate in an international meeting. Various world leaders would be meeting in Geneva to discuss banning the testing of atomic weapons, and the Women's Strike for Peace wanted to be there to represent the people of their respective countries who wanted a no-test agreement. They hoped to influence these talks by giving some insights on how atomic testing would affect the common people.

Both Coretta and Martin were very excited about the invitation, and Martin encouraged her to try to go. At first, she wasn't sure how she could arrange it. The meeting was to last a whole week, and she had to give a concert in Cincinnati on the Sunday the women were scheduled to return. She also wasn't sure that she could find someone to care for the children. But somehow, she was able to get all those things taken care of, and she joined the group of American women who went to Geneva.

It was a very interesting mixture of women. Some were professional women such as teachers. Others were mothers who had never been involved in politics before. Still others were women who had been active in the peace movement. Four of the women were black. When they arrived in Geneva, women from Scandinavia, Great Britain, Australia, and the Soviet Union joined the group.

What they all had in common was their concern about ending wars, and their support for a treaty that would ban the testing of atomic weapons. They felt that such a treaty was very important for the future of their children. They were also concerned about radioactive fallout from the testing of bombs, and how it affected their children's health. It was a very important matter to them, and they wanted it to be addressed.

After their arrival in Switzerland, the American women met with Arthur Dean, the United States representative. The women were disappointed with and quite insulted by the reception they got from him. His attitude was hard and unsympathetic, and he acted as if he was determined not to take them seriously—as if their request was so impossible that he would not even bother to consider it. They were further insulted by the fact that he was supposedly their representative, the American spokesman, whose function was to serve the wishes of the American people. Here were some American people expressing their wishes to him, and he was being rude to them. At the end, he walked out of their meeting, saying, "Why don't you go talk to [the Russians]?"[10]

And that is what the group did. Curiously enough, their meeting with the Russian delegation was much more friendly. A reception was held in honor of the group. Then they sat down and talked. This conversation was much more encouraging—at least they were listened to. Of course, they realized that the Russians knew just how to treat them so they would be impressed, even if they didn't mean any of the things they said. But still, the difference between the way the Russians treated them and the way their own representative did was amazing.

Five
Working for Civil Rights

By this time Martin was an international figure. He continued the practice he had established of going to the highest authority to present his requests for an end to the mistreatment of blacks. He spoke regularly with President Kennedy and his brother, Robert F. Kennedy, who was now the attorney general of the United States.

But at the same time, the United States government considered Martin a threat. Because of this, Martin Luther King, Jr., and all the people who worked with him were under FBI surveillance. This means that his home telephone was tapped, and frequently when he was away, recording devices would be placed in the locations where he would be staying. On several occasions Coretta was even told that Martin had been seeing other women, and in one instance a recording, allegedly of Martin with a woman, was sent to her. Martin and his colleagues were aware of what was going on. And Coretta refused to pay attention to any attempts to discredit

Martin or their marriage; she felt secure in their relationship.

Even with all the traveling and the fame and the busy schedules, Coretta and Martin still had three children to raise. Although Martin had to be away from home a great deal, he was wonderful with the children, and they adored him. When he was at home, it was a special occasion. Although Coretta was at home much more than Martin, she still traveled a great deal. But they had trusted friends who would take good care of the children until one or both parents returned. Whenever Coretta had to be away and left Martin at home to baby-sit, the children loved it because they would all have a wild time together. They loved to play on the bed and jump on top of him.

For black parents at that time, and especially for black parents in the South, it was very difficult to raise children in the dangerous and ugly climate of racism. It was even more difficult for Coretta and Martin, who were involved in fighting against racism—but still wanted their children to grow up without fear or bitterness in their hearts. Their activities in the Movement made it doubly difficult. But they did as good a job as they could.

There were times when Coretta and four-year-old Yoki might be driving past a playground in a white neighborhood. Yoki would say, "Mommy, look at the swings! I want to stop and swing. Please stop the car."[1]

Coretta would never stop; the playgrounds they passed were for white children only. But she would never tell that to Yoki at such a young age. She would say something like, "We have to get home and have lunch, honey," to distract her.

As Yoki got older, many times she would come

home and say to Coretta, "Mommy, I'm so tired of having people ask me, 'Are you Martin Luther King's daughter?' "[2] Coretta would then try to explain to her that people said these things because of the good her daddy was doing for all people, and because they thought well of him.

Yoki learned these lessons well. One day when she was about seven years old, she came home looking quite satisfied. She reported to Coretta that when the teacher left the room, she'd turned to the other children and said sternly, "Look, all I want is just to be treated like a normal child." Coretta laughed to herself and said, "Good for you!"[3]

Marty had his own special problems. His name evoked a certain hostility in some whites. This made it very hard for innocent Marty while he was growing up. Sometimes, when white children asked him what his father's name was, he would tell them he had forgotten because he was afraid they would beat him up.

One of the incidents with the children that was the most painful for Coretta and Martin involved Funtown, an amusement park that had just been built in Atlanta. It was advertised extensively, and the King children were attracted by the television commercials. They saw so many of them that they knew the commercial by heart. As they pleaded with Coretta and Martin to take them, Coretta and Martin would keep making excuses. It, too, was not for black children. Martin would say, "Not this week, children, I have to go on a trip," or something like that, week after week. Finally, Yoki, who was about six at the time, said, "You just don't want to take me to Funtown."

Coretta finally told her the truth in as kind a way as she could. "Yolanda," she said, "Funtown was built by people who decided that they did not want colored people to come there. They were not good Christians. You see, we are colored."

Yoki began to cry, and Coretta continued, saying the words that so many black parents had to tell their children: "Yoki, this doesn't mean you are not as good as those people. God made all of us and we are His children. He made some white, some brown, some black, some red, some yellow. He must have thought a lot of his black children because he made so many.

"Don't cry, because it won't be long before you can go to Funtown. This is what your daddy is doing in all his work; he is trying to make it possible for you to go to Funtown and any other place you want to go."[4]

This was the first time Yoki realized that as a black child there were places she could not go. She cried, yet it helped her to understand that her father was working to do something about these conditions—and that things could be changed. So in this way, his absences became more meaningful to her. Martin sometimes mentioned the Funtown situation in his speeches.

Many months after that conversation, in the spring of 1963, Funtown was quietly desegregated. Coretta and Martin decided to take Yoki, Marty, and Dexter, and they had a good time going on all the rides.

While they were there, a white woman came up to Coretta and asked, "Are you Mrs. King?" When Coretta told her she was, the woman said, "Oh, I'm so glad you are here. Is your daughter with you?" Coretta introduced Yolanda. The woman looked at her and said again, "I'm so glad you're here,"[5] and walked away.

Coretta was very glad that the children had been able to see that their father's work had brought relevant results in their own lives.

Coretta also felt that it was very important for black children to develop a healthy and positive attitude toward the color of their skin, instead of the negative attitude promoted by racist whites. She became particularly concerned about this when Yoki, at age seven, asked, "Mommy, why is it that white people are pretty and Negroes are ugly?"

"But, Yolanda, that's not true," Coretta said in dismay. "There are pretty people in all races."

"No," Yoki repeated emphatically. "White people are pretty and Negroes are ugly."

On a table nearby was a copy of *Ebony* magazine. Coretta picked it up, sat down with Yoki, and they looked through the pages together. As they came across photographs of black people, Coretta would say, "See her, see how beautiful she is!" or "Oh, isn't he handsome?" Yoki kept murmuring, "Mmm-hmm," and Coretta assumed that the lesson was working. But when they finished the magazine, Yoki said, "You know, colored people are pretty, and white people are ugly." Coretta exclaimed, "Oh no! That's not right either."[6] She had to start all over again.

Much later, in 1965, the Atlanta elementary schools became integrated, and Coretta and Martin wanted Yoki and Marty to transfer to an integrated school. When she discussed the matter of transferring with the children, they did not want to be the only two black children in an all-white school. So Coretta had an idea. She called Juanita Abernathy, whose three children were about the same age, and discussed the possibility of having all five children transfer to the same school. It turned out that Mrs. Abernathy's children felt the same apprehension as Coretta's did. So together, both families chose the Spring Street School, which they had been told was one of Atlanta's best public elementary schools. All five children were accepted, and they started school together.

As busy as Coretta was, she was still a wife and sometimes missed the "normal" life of having her husband and family together at home every day. She would have liked to have had more of Martin's attention, and there were indeed times when she would catch herself being a little resentful when, during his long absences from the family, he would forget things such as calling home to check on a sick child. But she taught herself to remember that Martin belonged not just to her and the children, but to the whole world. Therefore he could not be the kind of husband and father that she would have liked him to be. After all, she too was now a public figure, and could not appear to be a jealous or resentful wife. It was very important that people know her as the woman who encouraged and comforted Martin and was his good friend, and she made sure that was how she always presented herself.

From the beginning, Coretta considered her own role very important. She felt that she had a contribution to make to the cause, and involved herself in everything that Martin was doing. Besides, she felt very useful being able to relieve him of many of the responsibilities of home and church. She felt a sense of being needed and a security in their relationship, which gave her understanding and allowed her to be the kind of wife a man in Martin's position needed. And because she herself believed in the rightness of the cause, she was willing to make the necessary sacrifices. She often stated, "I am grateful that God has given me the opportunity to be the wife of this noble and dedicated leader. I consider it a great privilege to be able to share in all that he is doing and to play an important role in all that is happening in the world today."[7]

She told her children that they, too, were making a contribution to the civil rights struggle in their willingness to share their daddy. When they used to ask why he stayed away so much and was not at home like other daddies, Coretta would tell them that God has to have people to do His work, and that their daddy was one of God's helpers.

Every new development in the Civil Rights Movement was very distressing to many whites, and they fought back with violence in all the states in the South. It was an extremely dangerous time. There were bombs left at black people's doorsteps, and many who fought for the civil rights cause were injured, arrested, or even killed. But the blacks kept protesting in the nonviolent manner which Martin had taught them.

One of the things they protested was that only one out of one hundred black persons in Alabama was allowed to vote. The system there was designed so that blacks would find it difficult to vote. First, because the authorities knew that few blacks could read or write, they gave tests that were impossible to pass. Second, they established a set of very strict rules that any black person who did pass the test had to abide by. And third, sometimes they simply came right out and threatened the blacks.

In 1963, Martin and the SCLC decided that they would go to the governor of Alabama, a man named George Wallace, and petition him on this issue. They decided to do this by beginning to organize the people of Alabama and ending with a huge march from Selma to Montgomery, the state capital, where the governor's office was located.

There was one man in Alabama who was determined to defeat the blacks. His name was Eugene "Bull" Connor. He was the public safety commissioner of Birmingham, and he was a big, mean man who was famous for making sure all the laws of segregation were followed to the letter. Because of this, Martin knew the project would take a long time, so he set up headquarters in Birmingham.

Coretta, pregnant at the time, did her best to prepare herself for the idea that Martin might be away when the child was born. Even though she had gone through childbirth three times before, she would feel better if her husband was going to be there to share the experience. But Coretta recognized that it was important for Martin to be in Birmingham.

The Kings' fourth child, a daughter, was born on March 28, 1963. They named her Bernice Albertine after her grandmothers, and her nickname became Bunny. Martin was able to return to Atlanta to take Coretta to the hospital. But the next day, after the baby was born, he went back to Birmingham. Although he returned to Atlanta in time to take her home from the hospital, he had to return to his headquarters that same evening.

Coretta regretted that she couldn't be with him. She knew that he'd anticipated the possibility of going to jail, and she was concerned that she would not be there to comfort him. And that is exactly what happened.

On Good Friday, April 12, 1963, Martin was jailed during one of the sit-ins. But unlike other times when he had been jailed, Coretta did not hear from him, and neither she nor anyone else was able to get through to him. When Coretta had not heard from him by Easter Sunday, she became very worried about his safety. She was also burdened with the pressures of the phone constantly ringing, trying to take care of the children plus the new baby, and wanting to go to Birmingham to be near Martin.

She thought and thought about what she should do, and then remembered John F. Kennedy's words: "If there is anything I can do to help, please feel free to call on me." And while she was not trying to get Martin out of jail—for that would have defeated their purposes—she decided that if the president could intercede so that she could just talk to Martin, that would be sufficient.

When she called the White House, however, President Kennedy was away, and she had to leave word with Pierre Salinger, his press secretary. He promised to give the president her message and have him call her back.

While she was waiting, the Kings' friend Harry Belafonte called to say he was thinking about them and not to worry about Martin. When Coretta told him she hadn't heard from Martin and had just tried to reach the president, Belafonte became a little alarmed. But Coretta explained that all she wanted to do was tell the president how anxious she was about Martin's safety, and assured Belafonte that she had no intention of giving the impression that she was trying to get Martin out of jail. Then she told Belafonte about the problems she was having, and sounded very depressed. When he heard this, he told her to hire, at his expense, a secretary to take care of the phones and the paperwork, and a nurse to take care of the baby, and added that he would go to Birmingham with her.

While she was talking with Belafonte, her other phone rang. When she answered, a familiar voice said, "Mrs. King, this is Attorney General Robert Kennedy. I am returning your call to my brother. The president wasn't able to talk to you because he's with my father, who is quite ill. He wanted me to call you to find out what we can do for you."

Coretta explained: "I was calling because I am concerned about my husband. As you probably know, he is in jail in Birmingham, and he's been there since Friday. At this point, no one is able to see him. Usually they let him telephone me, but I have heard nothing from him directly, and I'm awfully worried. I wondered if the president could check into the situation and see if he's all right."

Robert Kennedy replied: "I'm sorry you have not been able to talk to your husband, but I'll tell you, Mrs. King, we have a difficult problem with the Birmingham officials. Bull Connor is very hard to deal with. But I promise you I will look into the situation and let you know something."

Coretta felt better after she hung up, because Robert Kennedy had seemed very concerned. That gave her the feeling there was a chance something might be done.

She heard nothing more until the next day, Monday, at about five in the afternoon, when there was a phone call from the president. He said, "I'm sorry I wasn't able to talk to you yesterday. I understand my brother called you. I just wanted you to know that I was with my father who is ill, and couldn't leave him." He asked how Coretta was and mentioned that he knew she'd just had a baby.

Coretta told him she was sorry his father was ill. She then told him that she was terribly concerned about Martin. President Kennedy told her that the FBI had been sent into Birmingham the previous night to check on Martin, and that he was all right. He added that he had just talked to Birmingham, and that Martin would be calling her shortly. "If you have any further worries about your husband or about Birmingham in the next few days, I want you to feel free to call me. You can get me or my brother or Mr. Salinger."[8] Coretta could hardly thank him enough for the relief he had brought to her.

Within fifteen minutes Martin called her. He told her that he was all right, but he sounded tired, as if he had lost all his energy. And then Coretta told him about her phone conversation with the president.

He said, "So *that's* why everyone is being so polite!"[9] He had suddenly been taken from his cell for exercise and allowed to take a shower, and been given a mattress and a pillow. Over the phone he told her to see that a statement was released to the press about her conversation with the president.

Coretta felt that President Kennedy's intervention helped the city officials realize they could not commit such inhuman practices without being exposed. She felt that President Kennedy sincerely cared about what happened to black people, and his concern and desire for justice encouraged them in their struggle.

Altogether, Martin was in jail for eight days. During this time, some white ministers placed a large advertisement in the local newspaper, calling Martin a troublemaker. Martin responded by writing a letter to them, in which he explained to these ministers and to the world why the fight against racism should not be delayed. Martin's letter was later published as an essay called *Letter from a Birmingham Jail*. It was reprinted in dozens of magazines and newspapers all over the world.

Finally, Martin was released on April 20. After his release, the next phase was planned. A lot of demonstrators were needed, but the leaders knew that most of the adults in Birmingham were afraid to demonstrate for fear of retaliation from the whites— they might even lose their jobs. So, for two reasons, it was decided that Birmingham's black children would be the perfect demonstrators. First, children would be less afraid. Second, when news reports showed innocent young children being arrested and taken to jail, the entire nation would see how cruel the Birmingham authorities really were.

After days of careful organization, assistance from parents and teachers, and instruction on how to act when arrested, black Birmingham schoolchildren from six to eighteen years old were prepared to demonstrate on Thursday, May 2. As they began to march, singing songs of freedom, police moved in to arrest them; but for four hours, more and more children continued to march, replacing those who were arrested. The next day, Bull Connor brought out the city's police dogs, and ordered the city's firemen to turn their water hoses on the children.

On television sets all across the country, people saw innocent children being knocked down by powerful streams of water from the hoses and chased by snarling police dogs. Newspapers and magazines at home and abroad also reported the events, with photos. This went on for four days, and by then, more than two thousand demonstrators had been jailed. The jails could not even hold all of the young prisoners.

These events were embarrassing to the country. President Kennedy sent a federal aide to Birmingham to encourage negotiations between Martin and the city's business leaders. Several days later, the merchants agreed to desegregate lunch counters and hire black workers.

In response, President Kennedy appeared on nationwide television to appeal to all Americans to eliminate segregation from the country. He stated that he would ask Congress to pass laws that would give *all* Americans the right to be served in public places such as hotels, restaurants, theaters, and stores. He said that no American in 1963 should have to endure denial of that right. Coretta and Martin were very pleased with President Kennedy's speech.

As he promised, on June 19, 1963, President Kennedy delivered a civil rights bill to Congress for passage. This bill banned segregation in all public interstate travel accommodations. It allowed the government to initiate lawsuits to force school integration, and to stop government funds to any federal program where discrimination took place. It also contained a provision that helped guarantee the right to register to vote by declaring that a person who had a sixth-grade education would be presumed to be literate. If Congress passed this bill, all of these things would become law.

Martin and all of the other civil rights leaders had no intention of letting this bill die in Congress. To show how much the public really wanted Congress to pass the bill, they decided to organize a demonstration in Washington, D.C. It would be a gathering of people from all over the country who wanted the bill to pass. It would show that black citizens were tired of waiting for fair treatment and equal opportunity. Civil rights groups and church groups nationwide notified people about the demonstration, called the March on Washington, which was scheduled to take place on August 28, 1963. During this time, Martin also began writing another book, about the Birmingham campaign. It was called *Why We Can't Wait*.

The day before the march, Coretta and Martin went to Washington, D.C., from Atlanta. In their hotel suite, Martin worked on his speech all night, not sleeping at all, revising it to fit into the eight minutes that had been allotted to him. When he finished it, he was extremely tired. Coretta read it and thought it was quite good.

On the day of the march, Coretta wanted very much to walk beside Martin, because she wanted the joy of being with him on that special day. But the planning council had decided that the march would be led by the top leaders. Coretta was not very happy about this. She felt that the wives of these leaders had shared the dangers and hardships, and some had been so extensively involved that they should have been granted the privilege of marching with their husbands and of completely sharing the experience. But they had to cooperate with the planning council's wishes.

Coretta marched with Ralph and Juanita Abernathy, Dr. Ralph Bunche, Lena Horne, and many other women and men who were fighters for the Movement. No seat had been provided for her on the speakers' platform, but she was lucky enough to get a seat almost directly behind Martin. She sat there looking at all the people, and it was the biggest crowd she'd ever seen in one place.

For hours, there were speeches and songs by many of the famous people of the day. Then Martin was introduced. The audience's response was warm and welcoming, and Coretta could tell that he was tremendously moved.

He started out with the written speech, and delivered it with great eloquence. When he got to the rhythmic part of demanding "freedom NOW" and "jobs NOW," the crowd caught the timing and shouted "NOW" together with him. Their response inspired Martin to abandon his written speech, and he spoke from his heart, his voice soaring out over the crowd and to all the world: "I have a dream . . ."

When the speech was over, Coretta clung to him

because of the mobs who were trying to get a glimpse of him. They got into a car that was taking Martin to the White House to have a conference with President Kennedy and other leaders. Coretta wanted very much to be present at the conference, but Martin had told her that it would be against protocol to have her come unless she had been previously invited. Again, she was not pleased. She rode with Martin to the White House gate, and then transferred to a taxi, which took her back to the hotel. That night, Coretta and Martin spent hours talking about how wonderful it all had been.

As black people became more determined to gain their rights, white segregationists in the South became more determined to keep things as they were, and they became more violent. An especially tragic result was the bombing of the Sixteenth Street Baptist Church in Birmingham less than three weeks after the March on Washington. The bombing took place on a Sunday morning, during Sunday school, and four innocent little girls were killed. Their names were Addie Mae Collins, Denise McNair, Carole Robertson, and Cynthia Wesley. Coretta and Martin were shocked, and Martin visited their families and preached at the funerals of the little girls.

Another tragedy took place on the afternoon of November 22, 1963. Coretta and Martin were both at home; Coretta was downstairs talking on the telephone, and Martin was upstairs watching television. He called her when he saw a news bulletin flash on the screen: President Kennedy had been shot in Dallas. They watched it together, and Martin was very quiet.

Then it was announced that the president was dead. Finally Martin said, "This is what is going to happen to me also. I keep telling you, this is a sick society."[10] Coretta could not say anything to comfort him. She could not say, "It won't happen to you," because she felt he was right. She could only hold him close.

Coretta was deeply affected by President Kennedy's death, even more so than she had been by Martin's stabbing in Harlem. As she watched the courageous Jacqueline Kennedy, President Kennedy's widow, and her small children, she kept thinking about Martin. For Martin's work was far more dangerous than the president's. It was as if, watching the funeral, Coretta was preparing herself for her own fate.

Vice President Lyndon Baines Johnson became the U.S. president, and urged that Congress quickly pass the Civil Rights Act in John F. Kennedy's memory.

For the Kings, that was the most important incident of the year. Martin was invited to the White House by President Johnson for the signing ceremony.

Soon afterward, the Kings received notification that Martin was the winner of the 1964 Nobel Peace Prize. This prize is awarded every year to the person who has made the greatest contribution that year to achieving world peace. The prize was presented to Martin at a formal ceremony in Oslo, Norway, attended by the king of Norway. Coretta, Martin's parents, and several of his aides were present.

Still, 1964 was the worst year in terms of violence. More people, both black and white, were working for the Movement. The protesters were escalating their activities, even involving the president and making him give them protection when it seemed necessary. The media coverage also increased, revealing the true nature of the white segregationists in the South, particularly in Mississippi and Alabama.

In June, three young men—one black and two white—had arrived in Mississippi to work with the Movement. Their names were Michael Schwerner, James Chaney, and Andrew Goodman. After being arrested on a speeding charge, they disappeared on June 21. Their burned-out car was found a few days later, and their bodies were found on August 4, buried in an earthen dam. Martin delivered the memorial service for these men.

That year, to raise funds for the SCLC and another fund established as the Goodman-Chaney-Schwerner Fund, Coretta began to give her Freedom Concerts again, in a format similar to the 1956 concert which she had given in New York. Newspaper reviews of the concerts praised the humanitarian goals of the fund-raising.

In this series of concerts, she told "The Story of the Struggle from 1955 to 1965" in an eight-part program of narrative and song. The first concert was given November 14, 1964, at New York City's Town Hall. The hall was filled, and the proceeds amounted to six thousand dollars. At first Martin didn't think the concerts would be successful in raising funds, but when they brought in more than fifty thousand dollars to the SCLC and its affiliates, he had to admit he had misjudged.

Coretta also continued to sing regularly with the choir of Ebenezer. Sometimes on the Sundays that Martin preached, he would ask her to sing some of his favorite hymns—particularly at Christmas and Easter.

MEETING MALCOLM X

Coretta had an opportunity to meet another emerging black leader, Malcolm X, the following year.

For leading a march to the Selma courthouse,

Martin and Ralph Abernathy were jailed for five days. During the five days, Coretta and Juanita Abernathy went to Selma to visit their husbands. On one of those days, there was a noonday rally that Coretta had not planned to attend. But Andrew Young, one of Martin's colleagues, found her and said, "You're going to have to come inside and greet the people, because Malcolm X is here and he's really roused them. They want to hear from you."

Coretta, however, was not in a speaking mood that day, and told him so. After some encouragement, however, she and Juanita went inside and spoke to the crowd. Coretta gave a short speech emphasizing the nonviolent approach and urging them to continue. After she spoke, she was introduced to Malcolm X. He asked her to convey his apologies to Martin for not being able to visit with him in jail, but that he had to catch a plane for London where he was to address the African Students' Conference. Coretta thanked him and promised to give Martin his message.

Although some of Malcolm X's Muslim principles were different from Coretta's Christian way of thinking, she was impressed with Malcolm's sincerity. When she visited Martin, she told him of their conversation, but their time together in the Selma jail was so limited that they didn't spend much of it discussing Malcolm. Ten days later, back in the United States, Malcolm was assassinated at a public rally in Harlem.

Malcolm's death, too, affected Coretta deeply. It seemed that there was tragedy to deal with every day.

In Alabama, plans continued to be made for the black citizens to demonstrate for voter registration. On Sunday, March 7, 1965, Alabama state troopers attacked 1,500 marchers as they tried to cross the Pettus Bridge on their way from Selma to Montgomery, the state capital. Martin was not participating in this march. Seventy to eighty marchers were injured, and television cameras were there to record the event. The photos and stories printed on the front pages of newspapers shocked people all over the country. The marchers went to court to get an order preventing the march from being stopped.

As these events were taking place, Coretta was in San Francisco, in the middle of a West Coast tour consisting of five SCLC fund-raising Freedom Concerts. She learned of the violence just before her performance, and was prepared to cancel if necessary and return home. But learning that Martin was safe, she went ahead with all five concerts as scheduled.

Meanwhile, President Johnson was growing tired of the conflicts that were going on in the South. He promised that a voting rights proposal was going to Congress in a few days. He also told Alabama Governor George Wallace that the state troopers should protect, not attack, peaceful demonstrators seeking to draw attention to their problems.

Finally, the marchers got a federal court ruling that the march could proceed, and on Sunday, March 21, the march from Selma to Montgomery began. It covered a distance of fifty-four miles, and took five days to complete. There were no attacks, and by the end of the march, 25,000 people had joined it.

Coretta had a commitment to speak at Bennett College in Greensboro, North Carolina, on the Sunday the march began, but she joined the march on Monday. On Wednesday night, the group was near their destination and camped out on the outskirts of the capital. There were so many famous entertainers there—including Harry Belafonte, Leonard Bernstein, Billy Eckstine, Nina Simone, Sammy Davis,

Jr., and dozens more—that they put on a spectacular show for the marchers. Then, Harry Belafonte and Martin asked Coretta to speak to the crowd.

Coretta told the marchers that they were now in the area where she had grown up, and that returning to Montgomery had a very special meaning to her. Then she spoke directly to the women about what this all meant for the future of their children, and recited some lines from the Langston Hughes poem, *Mother to Son*.

When they arrived at the capitol, Martin and a group of the leaders went inside to present a petition to Governor Wallace asking him to remove all obstacles to black voter registration in the state of Alabama.

The Voting Rights Act was signed into law by President Johnson on August 6, 1965. In a very short time, the number of black voters all across the South increased substantially.

After these gains had been made in the South, the leaders decided that it was time to address the issues of poverty and all other economic discrimination. Martin proposed that the SCLC expand its activities to the northern and western cities of the country, such as Baltimore, Philadelphia, Detroit, Los Angeles, and Chicago. Chicago was selected as the target city for the SCLC drive, to dramatize the issues and focus the attention of the nation on the problems of life in the black ghettos.

LIVING IN THE INNER CITY

In January 1966, the Chicago project started, and Coretta accompanied Martin on his trip there. He had decided not to stay at a hotel, but to rent a slum apartment so that he could share the life of the ghetto people. When they arrived, it was very, very cold.

Coretta had never seen anything like it. The apartment building had no lock on the front door. There were no lights in the hall, only one dim bulb at the head of the stairs. And the hallway smelled of urine because people would come in off the street to use it as a toilet.

Their apartment was on the third floor. They had to walk up two flights of shaky and broken-down stairs. When the owner had heard that Martin Luther King, Jr., would be the tenant, he had cleaned and painted the apartment. But that made no difference because the old paint had not been removed and the walls looked uneven and smeared.

There was a living room in front and then two bedrooms, a kitchen, and a bathroom. They had to go through the bedrooms to get to the kitchen. In the kitchen was an old refrigerator, which refused to work, and an old stove. There was hardly any heat in the apartment. Coretta tried to make it as livable as possible with used furniture and curtains and plants.

Coretta and Martin did not spend all of their time in this apartment; they both had to travel back and forth between Atlanta and their other commitments. But in the summer, they brought the children to Chicago to be with them.

Even though they had always lived as simply as they could at home, the children had never known such poverty. There were no trees or grass around. The only place outside for the children to play was in the dirt. There was always noise: from the traffic and the neighbors, both inside and outside the building. This was the everyday life for the children who lived there, and Coretta felt that it was a very meaningful experience for her own children.

The neighborhood people were glad to see the Kings, but at the same time they were embarrassed about their state. Martin told them how concerned he was and that he wanted to help them to try to improve some of the conditions. Eventually, with the help of some of the SCLC staff and supporters, they went to work on the building themselves, sweeping and taking out garbage. They encouraged the people not to pay rent but to use the money to fix up the building themselves.

Just as in Atlanta, people sought Martin out to talk to him—about their problems and their needs, such as heat, light, water, and food. Martin and Coretta even held meetings with the members of the teenage gangs in the area, trying to communicate the discipline of nonviolence. The gangs soon became very protective toward the Kings. Many of the gang members decided to practice nonviolence, and began demonstrating with members of the Movement. Coretta was proud of Martin's work with the Chicago gangs and felt that it was one of the greatest tributes to the nonviolent method and to Martin's leadership.

But Chicago was a very big city, and following a rally on Sunday, July 10, 1966, there was a riot the next night. Feelings could not be calmed, and the prevailing mood among the people was extreme desperation and anger.

The next day, Coretta was scheduled to speak on the subject of unity to a women's group at the YWCA. But because of the events of the previous night, it was not an appropriate subject. Later, at Coretta's suggestion, the women formed an organization to support the struggle in Chicago. It was named Women Mobilized for Change, and grew to well over one thousand members.

There were more riots in Chicago, and after they quieted down Coretta took the children back to Atlanta. Martin stayed behind to organize more marches and to meet with Mayor Richard Daley on the problems.

In early 1967, Martin began to speak out against the Vietnam War, which was beginning to escalate. Coretta was happy that he finally had an opportunity to speak publicly on the issue of peace, an issue she had been speaking out on for a long time. But many of Martin's colleagues in the Movement criticized him because they felt that his antiwar comments were politically based.

Coretta began to defend him. She explained that it would be hypocritical of Martin to believe in peace at home and not believe in international peace. It would be hypocritical of him to be a follower of the nonviolent philosophy and not speak out against war, and hypocritical of him to be a minister speaking out against the evils of society and not speak out against the evils of war. She pointed out that Pope Paul VI had visited America and spoke against war. Why is it, she asked, that when a black man, who is also a clergyman, speaks against it, he is criticized? Coretta was very adamant on this point.

Coretta also supported Martin through this year by helping him with his church work. They had had no chance to go away for a vacation during that time. The last vacation they had together was one week in 1965, when Martin went to Jamaica to speak at the University of the West Indies. Martin fell in love with the island, and returned there in January of 1967 to write his fourth book, *Where Do We Go from Here? Chaos or Community*. He also dedicated this book to Coretta.

She was able to join him for about a week, and it was a real vacation for her. Martin was writing for twelve to fifteen hours a day, but they had a lovely time together in their beautiful cottage on a cliff overlooking the Caribbean Sea.

For some reason, through 1967 and early 1968, Coretta and Martin had a premonition that something bad was going to happen. Martin talked about death frequently, although he wasn't morbid about it. On one occasion, when he was in Atlanta and on the way home, he sent Coretta some flowers from town. When she received them, she realized that they were artificial—and Martin had never sent artificial flowers before.

On March 23, 1968, Martin went on a trip through rural Georgia to meet the people who lived there. He took Marty and Dexter with him, and they were able to see all the hard work he did. Coretta was grateful that the boys had a chance to observe their father's activities.

Then, Martin received word that there was a sanitation workers' strike in Memphis, Tennessee. The workers were striking for better working conditions and wages, and Martin decided to go to Memphis and give his support. He made several trips to Memphis, where there were some problems caused by conflicts between the peaceful protesters and more militant individuals.

Coretta continued to make public appearances. On March 28, she was in Washington, D.C., to participate in a press conference with the president of the Women's International League for Peace and Freedom. She discussed the relationship of American domestic policy and the crisis in the cities as well as American involvement in Vietnam. Martin had also asked her to mobilize support from women's organizations for the Poor People's Campaign taking place in Memphis.

The last time Coretta and Martin saw each other was on the morning of April 3, as he left for a 7:00 A.M. flight to Memphis. The children, still sleeping, did not see him off. That evening, he called Coretta and at the end of their conversation, told her he would call her the following night.

LOSING MARTIN

The terrible phone call on the evening of April 4, 1968, came from Jesse Jackson: Martin had been shot on the balcony of the Lorraine Motel in Memphis. Jackson told Coretta that Martin had been shot in the shoulder and that she should come to Memphis immediately. Coretta reserved a seat on the next flight out, and after arranging for the children to be cared for, rushed to the airport.

At the airport, she was paged. When she answered the page, she was informed that Martin was dead.

She had seen it happen to so many others in the past few years. She and Martin had learned to live with extreme danger, had talked about the possibility of a violent death for either of them. Now it had happened. Coretta King had to call on all her years of bravery to maintain her strength and composure.

Their friends, family, and the entire world extended sympathy and support to Coretta and her young children. Coretta herself tried to find some meaning in this experience. Then she realized that Martin's death came so close to the anniversary of the death of Jesus, and remembered that Martin had often spoken of the meaning of Easter. He'd say that the moments of despair and doubt were the Good Fridays of life, but even in the darkest moments, something happens, and you realize that there is hope, and life, and light, and truth.

Yoki and the other children asked Coretta if they should hate the man who killed their daddy. Coretta replied, "No, honey. Your daddy wouldn't want you to do that."[11]

Martin's funeral was scheduled for Tuesday, April 9, 1968. On the preceding Saturday, Harry Belafonte had suggested that Coretta make some sort of public statement, and the press was invited to meet with them at Ebenezer.

There, Coretta thanked all her friends at the SCLC, Ebenezer, and throughout the world who had shown their support and assistance at that painful time. She told them that Martin would want SCLC to continue under the leadership of Ralph Abernathy, Andrew Young, and others.

Then she talked about Martin. She said, "My husband often told the children that if a man had nothing that was worth dying for, then he was not fit to live. He said also that it's not how long you live, but how well you live. He knew that at any moment his physical life could be cut short, and we faced this possibility squarely and honestly. My husband faced the possibility of death without bitterness or hatred. He knew that this was a sick society, totally infested with racism and violence that questioned his integrity, maligned his motives, and distorted his views. And he struggled with every ounce of his energy to save that society from itself.

"He never hated . . . and he encouraged us to do likewise, and so he prepared us constantly for the tragedy.

"I am surprised and pleased at the success of his teaching, for our children say calmly, 'Daddy is not dead; he may be physically dead, but his spirit will never die.' "[12]

It was there that Coretta let the people know that

her goal was to make sure that Martin's work would not die, and invited those who loved and admired him to join her in helping to fulfill his dream.

"The day that Negro people and others in bondage are truly free, on the day want is abolished, on the day wars are no more, on that day I know my husband will rest in a long-deserved peace,"[13] she said.

Six

Continuing the Work

The eyes of the entire world were on Coretta King after her husband's death, and sympathy was extended to her and her children from far and wide. President Johnson declared Sunday, April 6, a national day of mourning.

All was not peaceful, however; Martin's assassination set off riots in more than one hundred cities, in which forty-six people were killed.

Those who were observing Coretta saw her strength. She was under extreme stress, but to the public she projected an image of unfailing composure and dignity. In the days following the tragedy, through the funeral and the long hours of television coverage, she never cried in public.

Meanwhile, the march in Memphis was still scheduled to be held on Monday, April 8, as Martin had planned it. Harry Belafonte approached Coretta and gently asked if she would agree to go to Memphis and lead the march on that date, which was the day before Martin's funeral. Coretta immediately agreed.

Coretta took the children with her to Memphis, and the march took place without incident. Coretta gave a speech in which she spoke about Martin's qualities as a leader, husband, and father, and how he had been prepared to give his life. "How many men must die," she asked, "before we can really have a free and peaceful society?"[1]

The next day, she returned to Atlanta, where Martin's funeral was held at Ebenezer Baptist Church. The service was dignified and beautiful. Martin was buried at South View Cemetery. Coretta paid the bill for Martin's funeral herself, rather than depend on a donation to do so as was usually the case upon the death of an international public figure.

On April 29, the Poor People's Campaign began when Ralph Abernathy led a group of leaders representing poor people to Washington, D.C., for conferences with political leaders. Nine caravans of poor people arrived in Washington and erected a camp near the Lincoln Memorial, which they called Resurrection City.

Coretta was there, and spoke before this crowd. In a forceful speech, she called for a new community of brotherhood, and denounced racism, poverty, and war. She called on women to draw upon their resources of hidden strength and to form "a solid block of woman power" that might provide a new, creative approach to the crucial problems of the world. She said:

"Women, if the soul of this nation is to be saved, I believe that you must become its soul. You must speak out against the evils of our time as you see them. Those of us women who have been blessed with the privilege of bearing children have the sacred task of rearing them with a knowledge and understanding of our democratic heritage and the eternal values of love, justice, mercy and peace. As women and mothers, we have a common concern for the happiness of our children and their families, to unite our efforts throughout the world."[2]

She also spoke out against the war in Vietnam, calling it the most cruel and evil war in the history of mankind. She suggested that women speak out against the war and be willing to go to jail if necessary, adding that such protests would make an impact on the president and other national policymakers.

The eyes of the world were on her, and Coretta was emerging as an advocate of peace and supporter of "woman power." Articles were written about her in many newspapers and magazines, and she was frequently referred to as "tasteful" and "heroic." She continued to travel and make speeches, the topics of which were usually peace, brotherhood, and the power and strength of women. Many of her early appearances after the assassination were to fulfill commitments that Martin had previously made. For some of these speeches, she used notes that Martin had made. But as time went on, her own ideology came forth. She often compared the fight for civil rights and a better life at home with the struggle of developing countries, and always called for peace throughout the world. She scorned American involvement in Vietnam, and asked for amnesty for draft resisters and army deserters.

The SCLC was becoming plagued by internal problems, and there was an obvious conflict between Coretta and the organization. Their respective interests were changing: the SCLC was not ready to expand into the peace movement as Coretta was doing. Although she was not a part of the daily decision making, she still served as a board member. She let them know that she would do all she could for them as long as the SCLC remained committed to Martin's philosophy and work.

Coretta King had no intention of just being the silent widow of a great man. She knew there were people who would have preferred her to be silent. But she sincerely believed in the cause her husband had died for, and the causes that she spoke out on.

One of the first personal projects Coretta took care of following Martin's death was to go into seclusion—but not to mourn. Instead, she spent this time with a tape recorder, dictating the material for an autobiography, which was called *My Life with Martin Luther King, Jr.* There were many things that Coretta did not include in the book; she felt that it was too soon after Martin's death to reveal any problems they may have had with each other or with the groups they were part of. She preferred not to embarrass anyone, because that was not her purpose in writing the book. Besides, that wouldn't have been what Martin would have wanted.

My Life with Martin Luther King, Jr., was published in 1969, and received positive reviews as a personal narrative of their life together. The book was translated into several languages, was printed in a paperback edition, and Coretta made recordings of some of its chapters. When asked, she would say that she might write a sequel to it in ten or fifteen years.

When reporters asked Coretta about the rumor that her book, *My Life with Martin Luther King, Jr.*, had made her rich, she found the question amusing. She explained that if it hadn't been for the money that came from that book, she would have had to go to work. Martin's salary as copastor at Ebenezer had been only six thousand dollars a year, and Coretta asked the church to stop those checks on the very first Sunday after his funeral. Martin had had only a small insurance plan, and a large policy—that Harry Belafonte had arranged and paid for—which was intended for the children's education. As for Martin's book royalties and any other income, such as fees for his speeches and his writings, he had kept only enough for the expenses of feeding and clothing his family and paying the mortgage. The rest he gave to the SCLC. After his death the book royalties increased, but Coretta still had the family expenses.

Coretta's biggest project was to begin fulfilling the promise she had made at the press conference following Martin's assassination: to establish a proper memorial to Martin and all those who died in the nonviolent struggle. And she didn't mean just erecting a statue or a plaque. She wanted to restore his birthplace and build a living memorial—a place where there would be activity and life. It would include Martin's final resting place as well as a place where people could learn about nonviolence and the movement Martin had led.

First, Coretta formed a foundation to establish the memorial. On the foundation's board of directors and trustees were Coretta, former Vice President Hubert Humphrey, Senators Hugh Scott and Edward Kennedy, and Ralph Abernathy.

In February 1969, Coretta made a personal appeal to President Richard Nixon to propose legislation for a memorial park in Martin's honor. She hoped that the federal government could acquire the land for the park, and that she could carry on from that point and raise funds for construction of the learning center. The president seemed very enthusiastic at first, but later told her that he didn't think it was a good idea for him to propose that legislation. Instead, he offered the White House's help with some private fund-raising: some recordings of the White House birthday party for Duke Ellington, which it was suggested that the foundation sell. If sold, the records might raise $25,000. But since they needed 10 to 20 million dollars, Coretta declined the offer. They needed much more than albums to sell.

In March of 1969, Coretta received an honorary degree from Boston University, which was Martin's alma mater, and delivered Boston University's Centennial Founder's Day address. Again, she spoke of peace, poverty, and prejudice. Many of the listeners were reminded of Martin.

Actually, Coretta had a charisma similar to Martin's: everywhere she went, crowds of admirers appeared. She seldom relaxed while on the road and rarely joined in any local social events. But she always signed autographs and always shook hands. She continued to receive invitations from all over: in India, a ceremony was held for her, and in London, she was the first woman in history to preach at St. Paul's Cathedral during a regular Sunday service.

Coretta was absolutely sure that Martin was stronger in death than in life, because his death had caused the struggle for peace and understanding between people and nations to escalate. As far as Coretta was concerned, Martin was very much alive, and stronger than he ever was before.

Whenever she was back home in Atlanta, Coretta continued to sing in Ebenezer's choir, and to serve on various church committees. Her main source of relaxation was attending plays or concerts at Atlanta's Memorial Arts Center. She was not an athletic person, never having had a chance to pursue sports like tennis or swimming.

Over 250,000 pieces of mail—letters as well as

hundreds of invitations for Coretta to speak at universities, international conferences, and great churches of the world—arrived in the year following Martin's death. Each was read and answered if necessary. At first, there were checks and cash inside many of the letters. Later, after Coretta began her public speaking appearances, many of the letter writers, believing she was a millionaire, asked *her* for help and money.

Her home once again became a hub of activity. She established an office suite in the basement to handle the mountains of mail that came in daily. Her sister Edythe came from Pennsylvania immediately after Martin's death and served as one of Coretta's special assistants for years. Coretta hired several part-time employees and seven full-time ones, including a cook and a woman to help with the children, a man to handle the heavy chores, and an office staff that included five secretaries.

In her office, there was a small switchboard on her desk from which she could dial certain numbers and reach any part of her house. Many people who visited her were surprised that she even had an office and a staff. At first, they had no idea what she was doing.

Always highly organized, Coretta kept a schedule for every child so that she would be able to know in advance where each one would be. Whenever she had to travel, she would leave lists—one for each child, one for household maintenance, one for office routine—so that things would run smoothly in her absence.

When Coretta was in Atlanta, she rarely went outside her home. She became uncomfortable when she was recognized or stared at, so she stopped shopping in person. Instead, her assistants would purchase her clothes from downtown Atlanta department stores and bring them to Coretta at home, where she would select the items she wanted and have the rest returned. Groceries were ordered by phone and picked up by a young man on her house staff, or delivered by the grocer. Coretta's hair was often styled by a young woman on the part-time staff, or Coretta would sometimes go to a beauty salon in a shopping center near her home.

Coretta had been keeping as much material about Martin's work and the Civil Rights Movement as she was able to collect. She had hundreds of tape recordings of his sermons and all of his books and papers. She planned to transfer much of this to the exhibition hall in the King Center. In her home, she had a special closet containing all of Martin's awards and personal effects. All of his suits, shirts, and shoes, some still scuffed and muddy from marching, were neatly arranged inside. She never looked at them; rather, she planned to put some of these in the center as well. "Museums and memorials have kept other important people's things, so why shouldn't we preserve the things Martin left?"[3] she explained. Even the battered 1965 Chevrolet, the last car Martin owned, was in the garage, perhaps also to be an exhibit.

Naturally, Coretta needed the support and assistance of Martin's staff and followers to help her continue his work and to establish the memorial. To her surprise, she discovered that some of them—even some who considered themselves Martin's very close friends—made her feel as if they forgot that she needed them as much as, and perhaps more than, Martin ever did. When she noticed this, she thought that they were like moths hovering around a light— and disappearing when the light went out.

For these reasons and others, in spite of her visibility after Martin's death, Coretta became a more private person. Her smiles did not come as easily as before. When she spoke to reporters, she appeared very calm and sure, but not relaxed. Her words were chosen carefully so that they would not be misinterpreted. She still did not wish to discuss any problems that may have existed, because she did not want to cause damage or embarrassment to anyone. But in private, she was a lively person, with a warm sense of humor.

It was a difficult time socially and politically in the United States, and certain events directly affected Coretta's continuation of Martin's work. There was an increasing growth of black militancy which was born from the frustration black people felt, especially in the inner cities. In the face of this new attitude, some people were feeling that the philosophy of nonviolence that Martin promoted was becoming outdated and ineffective. Many of them were beginning to withdraw their support of the nonviolent programs Coretta felt she must carry on. Still others believed she no longer needed them for anything. And many of the celebrities who had followed Martin now seemed too busy to help her erect a memorial to their old friend.

When Martin's body was still out at South View Cemetery, Daddy King used to visit the grave frequently. Whenever he invited Coretta along, she would decline to go. She preferred to think that Martin was more alive than dead—for she saw proof of this every day, in the lives he had changed. In fact, she wanted the crypt removed from that cemetery as soon as possible. "There are nothing but *dead* people out there," she would say, "and I don't want Martin out there with all those *dead* people."[4]

Later, Martin's crypt was moved to an aboveground, parklike setting next door to Ebenezer, the first step in the preparation for the memorial park Coretta planned.

Coretta still had four young, energetic children to raise, and since she was their only parent, she made them the most important people in her life. When Martin was killed, Yoki was twelve, Marty ten, Dexter seven, and Bunny five. Just as they had to get used to being the children of a famous man, they now had to get used to being the children of a famous man who had been brutally killed. But Coretta remained a strong mother for them, and was available to them for open discussion of anything that was on their minds. She made sure they had discipline and a good education.

Considering the circumstances, the children were very well adjusted. At first, their classmates expected them to be stuck-up, but quickly found out that the King children were just like everybody else. So they were able to be normal children despite all the publicity and fame.

Yoki attended a predominantly white high school, and the others attended an ungraded school that permitted students to progress at their own pace. At thirteen, Marty was doing eighth-grade work; Dexter, at nine, was doing fourth-grade work; and seven-year-old Bunny was doing third-grade work.

Coretta gave each of them a weekly allowance. Yoki received $5.00, and the others $3.50. Out of this allowance, Coretta required each of them to pay their lunch fees during the school year, as well as their church pledges. Yoki's pledge was $1.00, Marty's and Dexter's 50 cents, and Bunny's 25 cents.

* * *

Coretta wasn't the only one who wrote a book about Martin. Many people were writing stories of his life. Some were written with Coretta's cooperation, others were written from research and interviews with people who worked with Martin. Some discussed in detail the issue and alleged evidence of Martin's possible extramarital affairs. Occasionally these authors were given media coverage.

While Coretta had long ago gotten used to these rumors, she knew that she would soon have to teach her children to do so. At the time, Yoki was the only one of the children who was old enough to understand, and one day, after hearing about it on television, she asked Coretta what "extramarital" meant.

Coretta said, "Don't you know what that means?" Yoki answered, "They're trying to say he was going with other women." Coretta replied, "That's exactly what they're saying."[5] Yoki immediately dismissed the idea, and continued listening to the rest of the news.

Coretta later explained to Yoki, and to the other children when they were older, that there were still people who weren't satisfied that their father was dead, and that these people were determined to kill him again by discrediting him. She warned the children that this was something that they would have to live with for the rest of their lives.

One thing that was not on Coretta's list of priorities was remarriage. Her marriage with Martin had been so fulfilling that she still had very special memories. Besides, she would always be Mrs. Martin Luther King, Jr., and her children would always be his children. To many, the King family was a symbol. And "What man wants to marry a symbol?"[6] she asked. Besides, no man could replace Martin in her or her children's minds or hearts.

In 1974, her family had to deal with another tragedy. On Sunday, July 1, during church services at Ebenezer, a deranged young black man (named Marcus Wayne Chenault) fired two guns into the crowd of four hundred worshipers. Martin's mother was killed as she played the organ.

Coretta often received suggestions that she run for some kind of political office or accept some kind of political appointment. But she always refused, because she felt that she'd then be a tool of the government. In later years, however, she became active in several political campaigns in Alabama, and in some cases gave concerts of freedom songs to raise funds for these. Her children often helped her on these projects.

Coretta continued her busy schedule of speeches and singing, and lending her name, time, and/or support to causes ranging from women's rights to full employment. She was a board member of the Southern Rural Action Movement, which established programs to provide people in small towns with better housing and jobs in light industries that the people developed and owned themselves. She was involved in the activities of the hospital workers' union Local 1199, in New York City, insisting that these workers, most of whom were black women, be treated and paid properly. Other such organizations included Clergy and Laymen Concerned About Vietnam, and the Commission of Economic Justice for Women. She deplored the apartheid situation and violence in South Africa, and often asked her elected representatives to vote for economic sanctions against South Africa. Her comments on such issues were often quoted in the press. She was interviewed for many articles, and she occasionally wrote articles about current topics.

But most of her time was spent speaking to people all over the world, asking for their donations for the Martin Luther King, Jr., Center. She had easy access to powerful people, and when she asked for money, contributions were often generous. She also wanted to have January 15, Martin's birthday, declared a national holiday. To get public support for such a holiday, she began to organize birthday celebrations for him in Atlanta.

There were many people who criticized Coretta, saying that she should have been raising the money to help poor blacks instead of to make a monument. Others said she should have used the money to help the SCLC.

It took a long time for her to make financial progress on the King Center. Every president had a different policy, and she learned not to expect too much from the White House. But in 1976, during Jimmy Carter's presidency, the center raised $3.5 million in federal construction funds. She was also able to get assistance from Ford Motor Company board chairman Henry Ford II. And from business, labor, and private foundations, another $4.7 million was raised. With the contributions growing, Coretta began to plan the center.

There would be programs for people of all ages. There would be an academy to teach adults how to read; a day-care facility for children from six months to five years of age; and a program to bring together students from the nation's top colleges and universities to study the philosophy of social change and to do fieldwork in social activism.

In June of 1978, there were a lot of celebrations in the King home. Yoki graduated from New York University with a master's degree in fine arts, and had plans to pursue a career in theater. She had already played the role of Rosa Parks in the 1977 television movie *King*. Marty graduated from Morehouse, and was trying to decide between religion and political science. There were people who expected him to be in the ministry, but he refused to be pushed. Dexter graduated from high school, and was considering a career in engineering, among other things. Bunny was still in high school, very athletic, and very interested in politics.

As the children got older and went off into their own separate interests, Coretta made sure to bring them together as much as she could. When all the children were in town, she would make a point of having Sunday breakfast together. They would have a meditation session and then talk about whatever was on their minds. Coretta got strength from those gatherings. And the children had a great deal of respect for her; they knew that whenever they had a problem or a question, they could talk to her about it. They were all very open and trusting with each other, and they admired Coretta's strength and determination.

THE MARTIN LUTHER KING, JR., CENTER FOR NONVIOLENT SOCIAL CHANGE

In that same year, Coretta's strength and determination were now evident in the almost-completed memorial to Martin, which she officially named The Martin Luther King, Jr., Center for Nonviolent Social Change. She insisted that "Nonviolent" be part of the name.

The programs and facilities of the King Center were developed in a four-phase plan. Phase I was the restoration of Martin's birthplace, 501 Auburn Avenue. This was completed in January 1975. Phase II was the Martin Luther King, Jr., Community Center, built by the city of Atlanta, at 450 Auburn Avenue. Phase III, the Permanent Entombment and the Inter-Faith Peace Chapel, was dedicated in 1977. Phase IV, the Freedom Hall Complex, was completed in 1981.

Present at the Freedom Hall groundbreaking ceremonies in October 1979 were Daddy King, Atlanta's mayor Maynard Jackson, Henry Ford II, Andrew Young, who was now a former United States ambassador to the United Nations, and Vice President Walter Mondale.

By 1980, there were people who were openly criticizing both Coretta and the King Center. A local radio reporter broadcast several investigative reports, in which he questioned certain aspects of the center's development, including where all the money went. He interviewed dozens of people and did a great deal of research. But he could find no real evidence that any of the King Center's funds had been misappropriated.

Still, the criticisms continued, many from people who lived in the neighborhood around the center. Some of them felt that the center should be doing more to help the poor and elderly. They complained that the center did not stay in tune or in touch with the underprivileged, the underpaid, the "regular" people. If the King Center owned so much property, they asked, why didn't they tear down some of the slums and replace them with decent housing? They felt that was what Martin would have wanted done. Others, mostly younger people, were not familiar with the center at all. Still others commented that Coretta was becoming too partisan to the Democratic party and Jimmy Carter, whom she publicly endorsed in the 1980 presidential election. Then, there were people who worked with her at the King Center, who complained that her desire to control every small decision and every aspect relating to Martin's life, works, and image made her very difficult to work with.

But Coretta calmly ignored all the critics, never dignifying their comments with a response, and continued doing her work and moving forward. Of course, there were also those who felt that the King Center was doing important work. They cited the center's President's Program, which gave the people the opportunity to discuss and work with their government representatives on solutions to important social issues. Through this program, many important issues—such as support of the Equal Rights Amendment and the causes of the labor movement—were addressed, and conferences, such as the White House Conference on Families, were established. Coretta was the deputy chairperson of this organization. Through the President's Program, Coretta was allowed to attend the United Nations as the first voting public delegate.

Despite the varying opinions, everyone had to admit that the King Center was an impressive structure. The Freedom Hall Complex was officially opened on January 15, 1982, Martin's fifty-third birthday. Coretta was extremely proud. Dignitaries from all over the world came to the opening, and Coretta received letters of congratulation from President Ronald Reagan and former President Carter.

The King Center is a striking group of modern buildings on landscaped grounds. As Coretta wished, Martin's crypt is now elevated, and surrounded by a long, rectangular reflecting pool. The Eternal Flame is placed in front of the crypt area, and the arch-covered Freedom Walkway runs parallel to the pool.

The Freedom Hall Complex forms a complete rectangle around the crypt. At one end of the complex is an all-faiths chapel. At the other end is a three-story building, which houses the administrative offices, exhibition hall, and the King Library and Archives. Freedom Hall itself contains an international conference center with meeting rooms, a gift shop, an auditorium, and a film screening room.

There is no admission fee to the center; its only income from visitors comes from the gift shop. Coretta and the board continue to accept financial assistance from city, state, and federal governments, corporations, foundations, and individuals.

The whole King family helped with the running of the center. Yoki became the director of the Cultural Affairs Program. She was responsible for creating programs in the performing arts and demonstrating how nonviolence can be taught through the arts. Marty worked to get sponsors for a concert at New York's Radio City Music Hall to benefit the center. Bunny, while studying for theology and law degrees, helped to organize the southeastern region of the country to petition for Martin's birthday to become a national holiday. Dexter became executive producer of the "King Holiday" album, and in 1989, Coretta appointed him to the post of president of the King Center. However, a few months later, he resigned, preferring to pursue a career as a businessman.

* * *

On November 11, 1984, Daddy King died of a heart attack in Atlanta. Despite the many tragedies in his life, he had seen a large part of his son's dream come true, had written an autobiography, and had a family he could be proud of. Vice President George Bush and former President Jimmy Carter were among the speakers at his funeral. He had been the pastor of Ebenezer Baptist Church from 1931 to 1975.

In the 1980s, Coretta continued to insist that the United States government pass legislation endorsing economic sanctions against the South African government. The House of Representatives had passed the bill, and it was now before the Senate. It was the first bill against South Africa that had a chance of being passed.

The day before the Senate was to vote on endorsing these sanctions, Coretta, Marty, and Bunny went to Washington, D.C., to join a demonstration at the South African embassy. All three were handcuffed, arrested, and jailed overnight. But so had over 2,500 other protesters in the preceding seven months. Although most protesters were released, Coretta and the children chose to spend the night in jail.

A NEW HOLIDAY

Finally, Coretta's efforts bore fruit in another way: Martin's birthday finally became a national holiday, the first one to honor a black American. January 20, 1986, was to be the first observation of the federal holiday commemorating Martin's birthday. Coretta made an attempt to tie the event to the movement for world peace. In a luncheon address before the National Press Club, she asked for a United Nations resolution urging all nations in conflict at that time to cease hostilities on that date. They included South Africa, Vietnam, Cambodia, Afghanistan, Nicaragua, El Salvador, Lebanon, and the Soviet Union.

In 1986, Coretta made a ten-day visit to South Africa for the installation of Desmond Tutu as Anglican archbishop of Cape Town. While there, she planned to visit Winnie Mandela, wife of the then jailed activist Nelson Mandela; State President P. W. Botha; and Mangosuthu Buthelezi, the leader of South Africa's six million Zulu people. Mrs. Mandela warned that she would not meet with Coretta if Coretta met with either of the other two.

In the end, although both President Botha and Buthelezi accused her of being manipulated, Coretta decided to cancel the two meetings and meet Winnie Mandela instead. They spent over an hour together, and each was moved by the other's strength, courage, and sacrifices. Coretta also met with black businessmen and antiapartheid leaders. But she was not prepared for the different antagonisms she found, and admitted that the political situation there was more complicated than she realized.

In the meantime, the House and the Senate had both agreed on a set of sanctions against South Africa, and the bill was now before President Reagan—who had promised to veto it. It would ban new American investments and bank loans to South Africa, stop imports of South African goods, and end airline service between the two countries. When Coretta returned from her trip, she visited the White House and made a personal plea to President Reagan urging that he not veto the bill. She also suggested a program be drafted to ensure that the people of South Africa would not be hurt by the sanctions.

* * *

In the late 1980s, Coretta continued her activities for the causes she believed in. Her commitments had not changed much since the 1960s; for her, the causes were still relevant.

There are people who feel that Coretta is representing an outdated way of thinking in a time when the issues are different. Often when she speaks to groups of young students and talks of the Civil Rights Movement and Martin's work, young black people don't relate to what she's trying to say.

But she points to increasing incidents of racial violence in American cities as proof that her work will *always* be relevant. Toward this end, she plans to continue training a new generation in Martin's philosophy of bringing about social change. She also plans to produce programs and videos about nonviolence for general audiences of all ages, and hold seminars for world leaders to study nonviolence. She has no intention of going quietly away—not while there is work to be done.

Even among those people who criticize Coretta Scott King, there is respect. She is respected because she has kept her family intact, she has sustained the Martin Luther King, Jr., legacy, and she has built an institution to celebrate the Civil Rights Movement and to keep its lessons alive and functioning. No one person in history has ever done that.

Throughout her life, Coretta Scott King has backed up all of her words with commitment and action. By so doing, she has provided an example of human determination for men and women of any age, and all over the world, to follow.

Source Notes

Chapter One: Growing Up

1. Coretta Scott King, *My Life with Martin Luther King, Jr.*, p. 27.

Chapter Two: Education

1. Coretta Scott King, *My Life with Martin Luther King, Jr.*, p. 34.
2. Ibid.
3. Ibid., p. 43.
4. Coretta Scott (King), "Why I Came to College."
5. King, *My Life with Martin Luther King, Jr.*, p. 49.

Chapter Three: Courtship and Marriage

1. Coretta Scott King, *My Life with Martin Luther King, Jr.*, p. 52.
2. Ibid., p. 53.
3. Ibid.
4. Ibid., p. 54.
5. Ibid.
6. Ibid.
7. Ibid., p. 55.
8. Ibid., p. 56.
9. Ibid., p. 63.
10. Ibid.

Chapter Four: Early Years with Martin Luther King, Jr.

1. Coretta Scott King, *My Life with Martin Luther King, Jr.*, pp. 100–101.
2. David J. Garrow, *Bearing the Cross*, New York: Vintage, 1988, p. 12.

3. King, *My Life with Martin Luther King, Jr.*, p. 145.
4. Ibid., p. 146.
5. Ibid., p. 191.
6. Ibid.
7. Ibid., p. 196.
8. Ibid.
9. Ibid., p. 197.
10. Ibid., p. 210.

Chapter Five: Working for Civil Rights
1. Coretta Scott King, *My Life with Martin Luther King, Jr.*, p. 213.
2. Ibid., p. 210.
3. Ibid., p. 211.
4. Ibid., p. 213.
5. Ibid., p. 214.
6. Ibid., p. 215.
7. Coretta Scott King, "The World of Coretta King."
8. King, *My Life with Martin Luther King, Jr.*, pp. 225–226.
9. Ibid., p. 227.
10. Ibid., p. 244.
11. Ibid., p. 321.
12. Ibid.
13. Ibid., p. 327.

Chapter Six: Continuing the Work
1. Coretta Scott King, *My Life with Martin Luther King, Jr.*, p. 329.
2. Phyl Garland, "Coretta King: In Her Husband's Footsteps."
3. Charles L. Sanders, " 'Finally, I've Begun to Live Again.' "
4. Ibid.
5. Ibid.
6. Ibid.

Bibliography

Books

King, Coretta Scott. *My Life with Martin Luther King, Jr.* New York: Holt, Rinehart & Winston, 1969.

Periodicals

"Coretta King: Keeping the Dream Alive." *Ebony,* January 1980.
"Coretta King Pushes Reagan to OK S. African Sanctions after Recent Visit There." *Jet,* October 6, 1986.
"Coretta King Urges World Peace on King's Birthday." *Jet,* October 4, 1985.
Friedman, Saul. "Mrs. King: Peace Warrior." *Detroit Free Press,* November 29, 1965.
Garland, Phyl. "Coretta King: In Her Husband's Footsteps." *Ebony,* September 1968.
Greenwald, John. "Into the Racial Maelstrom." *Time,* September 22, 1986.
Gulliver, Hal. "Coretta Scott King: 'Moral Leadership, from the Young People, Is Our Real Hope.' " *Today's Health,* November 1973.
[King], Coretta Scott. "Why I Came to College." *Opportunity,* Spring 1948.
―――. "My Dream for My Children." *Good Housekeeping,* June 1964.

———. "The World of Coretta King." *New Lady,* January 1, 1966.

"King Family Arrested and Jailed for Embassy Protest." *Jet,* July 15, 1985.

Leavy, Walter. "A Living Memorial to the Drum Major for Justice." *Ebony,* February 1983.

Leifermann, Henry P. " 'Profession: Concert Singer, Freedom Movement Lecturer.' " *New York Times Magazine,* November 26, 1972.

[Morrison, Don]. "NEA President Don Morrison Interviews Mrs. Martin Luther King, Jr." *Today's Education,* January 1972.

Norment, Lynn. "Coretta Scott King: The Woman Behind the King Anniversary." *Ebony,* January 1990.

"Once the Woman behind the Martyr, Coretta King at 50 Becomes a Power on Her Own." *People Weekly,* February 20, 1978.

Osborne, John. "Dr. King's Memorial." *The New Republic,* October 11, 1969.

Ruffin, Frances. "Yolanda King: 'The Theater Is My Ministry.' " *Redbook,* September 1979.

Sanders, Charles L. " 'Finally, I've Begun to Live Again.' " *Ebony,* November 1970.

Shannon, Margaret. "The Widow's Might." *Atlanta Journal & Constitution Magazine,* February 1, 1976.

"The Woman Behind Martin Luther King." *Ebony,* January 1959.

"The Widows: Keeper of the Dream." *Newsweek,* March 24, 1969.

Walker, Alice. "The Growing Strength of Coretta King." *Redbook,* September 1971.

Williams, Juan. "Coretta's Way." *The Washington Post Magazine,* June 4, 1989.

Wortham, Offie. "I Have a Dream . . ." *Atlanta Magazine,* September 1980.

Index

Abernathy, Juanita, 51, 79, 88, 92
Abernathy, Ralph, 51, 63, 67, 88, 92, 100, 103, 106
Anderson, Walter F., 29, 30

Bartol, Mrs., 32, 33
Belafonte, Harry, 59, 60, 83, 93, 94, 100, 102, 106
Bennett, Mattie, 19
Bernstein, Leonard, 93
Botha, P. W., 120
Bunche, Ralph, 88
Burroughs, Fannie, 16
Bush, George, 119
Buthelezi, Mangosuthu, 120

Carter, Jimmy, 114, 117, 119
Center for Nonviolent Social Change, Inc., Atlanta, 9, 11, 109, 114–118
Chaney, James, 91
Civil Rights Movement, 10–11, 52–72, 75–98, 102–105, 121
Collins, Addie Mae, 89
Connor, Eugene "Bull," 82, 84, 86

Daley, Richard, 97
Davis, Sammy, Jr., 93
Dean, Arthur, 74

Eckstine, Billy, 93
Ellington, Duke, 59, 107

Ford, Henry, II, 114, 116
Freedom Concerts, 23, 91, 93

Gandhi, Mohandas K., 55, 64, 65
Goodman, Andrew, 91

Horne, Lena, 88
Hughes, Langston, 94
Humphrey, Hubert, 106

Jackson, Jesse, 99
Jackson, Maynard, 116
Johnson, Lyndon B., 90, 93, 94, 102

Kennedy, Edward, 106
Kennedy, Jacqueline, 90
Kennedy, John F., 71, 75, 83–87, 89–90
Kennedy, Robert F., 71, 75, 83–84
King, Alberta, 45, 46, 113
King, Alfred Daniel, 46
King, Alveda, 46
King, Bernice Albertine "Bunny," 82, 111, 115, 118, 119
King, Christine, 42
King, Coretta Scott
    assassination of Martin Luther King, Jr. (1968) and, 10, 99–101
    Center for Non-violent Social Change and, 109, 114–118
    children and, 69, 76–78, 111, 115, 118
    Civil Rights Movement and, 10–11, 54–61, 65–72, 75–97, 102–105, 121
    courtship of, 35–47
    education of, 18–34
    growing up, 13–17
    marriage of, 47–48
    music and, 22–24, 29–31
    religion and, 36
King, Dexter Scott, 72, 78, 98, 111, 115, 118
King, Martin Luther, Jr., 9–11, 36–72, 75–101
King, Martin Luther, Sr., 37, 46–48, 71–72, 110, 116, 119
King, Martin Luther "Marty", III, 63, 69, 77–79, 98, 111, 115, 118, 119
King, Naomi, 46
King, Yolanda "Yoki," 52, 56, 58, 69, 76–79, 100, 111, 112, 115, 118

"Letter from a Birmingham Jail" (M. L. King, Jr.), 85

McMurry, Grandfather, 16, 22
McMurry, Grandmother, 16
McNair, Denise, 89
Malcolm X, 91, 92
Mandela, Nelson, 120
Mandela, Winnie, 120
Mann, Horace, 29
Mays, Benjamin, 36
Mondale, Walter, 116
My Life with Martin Luther King, Jr. (C. S. King), 105

Nehru, Jawaharlal, 64
Nixon, E. D., 53
Nixon, Richard, 62, 72, 106–107
Nkrumah, Kwame, 61

Parks, Rosa, 53, 115
Paul VI, Pope, 97
Powell, Mary, 36–38, 41, 45, 46

Reagan, Ronald, 117, 120
Robertson, Carole, 89
Robeson, Paul, 30
Robinson, Jo Ann, 54

Salinger, Pierre, 83, 85
Schwerner, Michael, 91
Scott, Bernice McMurry, 14, 15, 19–22
Scott, Cora, 15–16

Scott, Edythe, 14–19, 22, 24–26, 108
Scott, Hugh, 106
Scott, Jeff, 15–17
Scott, Obadiah, 14–15, 17, 19–22, 47
Scott, Obie, 14–18
Simone, Nina, 93
Southern Christian Leadership Conference (SCLC), 61, 65, 66, 81, 91, 93, 94, 96, 100, 104–106, 114
Stride Toward Freedom (M. L. King, Jr.), 62–63
Student Non-Violent Coordinating Committee (SNCC), 68–69, 72

Tutu, Desmond, 120

Wallace, George, 81, 93, 94
Wesley, Cynthia, 89
Where Do We Go from Here? Chaos or Community (M. L. King, Jr.), 97
Why We Can't Wait (M. L. King, Jr.), 87
Williams, Olive, 22–23, 29
Wormley, Bertha, 32–33

Young, Andrew, 92, 100, 116